Henry Barnes
A Constellation of Human Destinies

Henry Barnes

A Constellation
of Human Destinies

Edited by John Michael Barnes

Adonis *Press*

Published by Adonis Press
321 Rodman Road
Hillsdale, New York 12529
www.adonispress.org

ISBN 978-0-932776-38-9

This publication was made possible through the generous
support of the Rudolf Steiner School.

Cover design by Mary Giddens

Printed in the United States of America

Contents

Introduction

As soon as youth awakens to selfhood, it quite rightly sees itself as separate, unique, and independent. From the vantage point of old age, however, one begins to see one's life as part of a much larger picture. This unusual book is a mosaic, an attempt to shed light on the life and destiny of Henry Barnes from many different points of view.

The book begins with Henry Barnes, at 96, recounting his childhood and fateful meeting with anthroposophy and Waldorf education. After describing the events that led him to his life's task, he gives a brief overview of his work and his writings. Then the perspective changes and we catch glimpses of him through the eyes of others: old friends, former colleagues and students, and his own two children. We then again hear from "the old man" as he speaks about his old age and the two life companions whose destinies he sees as inseparable from his own: his wife Christy MacKaye Barnes, and her sister Arvia MacKaye Ege. Thus, in both its authorship and content, this book represents a larger constellation of destinies clustered around its lodestar, Henry Barnes.

John Michael Barnes

* * *

The "lodestar" wishes to express his gratitude and appreciation for the insightful and loving work of John Barnes—with the support and encouragement of his sister, Marion MacKaye Ober—without whom this volume would never have come into existence.

Henry Barnes

A Constellation of Human Destinies

In this volume we share the paths of destiny which led the individuals whom we shall meet to truly find each other. We will start with the autobiographical life-story of the one who is still here on Earth today and who can serve as our recording scribe.

As it is the intention of this book to place my own life into the broader context of a greater constellation of destinies, I welcome with special gratitude the memories of others whose contributions complement my own and are gathered up in the second section of this book.

I then resume my narrative, this time with an account of my old age. This is followed by the life-sketch through which we meet my beloved life-companion, Christy MacKaye Barnes, poet and artist of the spoken word, whose being also speaks to us out of the loving memories of her children, John Michael Barnes and Marion MacKaye Ober. This then leads us on to meet Christy's older sister, Arvia MacKaye Ege, who played a significant part in helping Rudolf Steiner become a living presence in the Western World today.

We welcome you, dear Reader, to join us on our pilgrimage.

Childhood and Youth

It was on August 12, 1912, on Manhattan Island in the heart of New York City that I entered life as the first child and oldest son of Henry Burr Barnes and Mabel Irving Jones who had been united in marriage the previous year. As my parents' names indicate, it was my good fortune to unite two strands of American history in my family background. Aaron Burr (1756–1836) served as Vice-President under Thomas Jefferson and played a significant role in the years following the American Revolution. Unfortunately, he is chiefly remembered today for mortally wounding Alexander Hamilton in a duel. Washington Irving (1783–1859) was the first American writer to achieve recognition in the international literary community. He served as Ambassador to Spain and is known especially for his short stories "The Legend of Sleepy Hollow" and "Rip Van Winkle" as well as for his *History of Christopher Columbus*. New York City, including Brooklyn, had been home to the families of both my parents for several generations, and I remember my mother saying that when, as a girl, she had lived on Washington Square, everything north of 59th Street was "country." When she later attended Columbia University as one of their first women students, she traveled through farmland by coach to reach the University at the northern end of Manhattan Island.

My father was a gentle, kindly man who, when he graduated from Yale College in 1893, was advised by his father to study law rather than to enter on a business career, as American business, at that time, was experiencing a downturn. As a result, my father became a lawyer whose clients were primarily indigent immigrants in need of legal assistance. As I return in memory to my father, one experience, in particular, recurs with special fondness. I remember how he would take me by the hand and, together, we would walk the few blocks from our home to the East River to watch the tugboats hauling the barges to the docks and warehouses on the Brooklyn shore.

Mother as a young woman

Family Photograph

Reading

Repairing

Seabright

In these early years, during the summer holidays, my parents would rent a home either on the Jersey shore or on Long Island, and the photograph included here not only shows the old author as a chubby one-year-old but also shows his parents on the verandah of their summer home in Seabright, New Jersey, and conveys a sense of the loving attention with which they welcomed their young son.

When I was four years old I was joined by my next younger brother Edward who was followed a year later by Alfred, and with Alfred's arrival the Barnes family was complete.

Characteristic of our mother was her deep-seated respect for each individual's right to be treated fairly as a human being no matter what his or her outer circumstances might be. She had, for instance, become aware that there were countless children, often hidden away in the back rooms of New York City tenements, who were in need of care, of which their parents were either unaware, or were unable to provide. The realization of such human needs had led her to help establish an organization dedicated to finding practical ways to provide the help that was needed. The organization came to be known as the Association for the Aid of Crippled Children. The Association attracted the help and support of a growing community of New York citizens and, over time, led to an annual fund-raising initiative which became a popular social event, warmly supported by the municipal authorities. While I was growing up, our family had a cook and a butler. My mother made it very clear to us children that these servants were to be treated with respect and addressed courteously with "Mrs." and "Mr."

Alfred and Edward to my right and left

It was primarily my mother's decision to enroll me, at the age of six, as a first-grader in the Lincoln School of Teachers College which had opened its doors the previous year on Park Avenue and 67th Street, opposite the Armory. And it was decisive in my life's destiny that another little boy also entered the first grade at the same time. Peter Stockton and I became lifelong friends, although Peter's life was to end tragically thirteen years later.

The Lincoln School and the Francis Parker School in Chicago were the two schools that pioneered the educational philosophy of John Dewey which came to be known as "Progressive Education" in the middle and later years of the 20th century. Generously supported by the Rockefeller family, whose children also attended the Lincoln School, the school attracted gifted, creative teachers and became a thriving institution in New York life at that time. The Lincoln School broke radically from the more traditional education that drew on the humanistic/academic approach especially characteristic of British education. Lincoln refused to teach Latin and Greek and included the arts in its curriculum.

In a historical perspective, I vividly remember a morning in November 1918 when our first grade piled out of our classroom to celebrate what we were told was the end of the World War into which the United States had entered the previous year. But, to our dismay, we were shepherded back into the classroom and told that it was a "false armistice" that had been mistakenly announced. A few days later, we were decorously led to the official celebration of the actual armistice on November 11th.

Peter and I wended our way together from year to year until seventh grade when the school skipped me from seventh to ninth grade where I was confronted by such powerful individuals as Jack Apple and such charming young maidens as Martha Knox. It was also during these years—thanks once again, to the Rockefellers, I am sure—that the Lincoln School moved up to Morningside Park and 123rd Street into its own, newly constructed school building that now housed a well-equipped gym and impressive auditorium and stage. In consequence, what had formerly been a short hike down Park Avenue from my home on 91st Street now became a ride on a double-decker Fifth Avenue bus up to Morningside Drive. In those days, you climbed a curving stair at the back of the bus, which led up to the open upper deck. And, unless it was pouring rain, every sturdy young New Yorker wanted to sit on the front seat, where you hung onto the rail and charged ahead as the bus careened through the traffic.

An event which comes back to me from my high school days was when we gathered in the school auditorium to devise a "cheer-leading" formula in support of our soccer and basketball teams. I was, I think, a tenth grader at the time and was inspired to dash to the stage to lead the crowd in a roaring: "LI, LI, LI – N! CO, CO, CO L – N! Lincoln! Lincoln! Lincoln!"

I also remember, with sincere gratitude, forging a pair of iron andirons in workshop class; experiencing an inner awakening through mathematics under Mr. Merrick, our outstanding high school math teacher;

and receiving a solid foundation in the German language from Fräulein Holtz, our German teacher.

When I was eleven years old, our mother took an initiative which transformed our lives. She bought a farm north of Stonington, Connecticut, which became our true home, even though we continued, for some time, to live for most of the year in the city. The farm came to be known as *Boulderwood* because of the granite boulders that studded the landscape. Mother engaged a fine Finnish farmer, Mr. Aalto, to manage the farm. The Aaltos lived next door, at the entrance to the farm, and, when I could, I helped Mr. Aalto in the barn. Mr. Aalto taught me to churn butter and sometimes even to milk. But my special joy was to build a stone wall to enclose the kitchen garden and then to prepare the ground across the road to be my vegetable garden where I raised vegetables that I peddled in the village of Stonington. It was also at this time that I became President and CEO of the Barnes Brothers Berry Company in which my brothers Edward and Alfred were the principal work force, who were generously rewarded by being allowed to eat as many blackberries as they wanted. The blackberry patch was down the lane behind the barn. We also sold the berries, along with the vegetables, in the village.

The Barnes Brothers

I remember a dramatic moment in the farmyard behind our house when my mother dashed out and thrust herself between Mr. Aalto and another, visiting farmer who were on the verge of a fight. Though both men were brandishing pitchforks, they had no choice but to submit to my resolute mother. The battle was averted and each man went on about his own business.

Thanks to a generous birthday gift from my parents, as a young teenager I was given a single-masted racing sloop which was moored near the dock of the Country Club, to which my family belonged, where we played tennis and went swimming, at the west end of Stonington harbor. Stonington harbor opened into Fisher's Island Sound which led further to the greater reaches of Long Island Sound to the southeast and to Narragansett Bay to the northeast which became my home-waters. My younger brothers Edward and Alfred shared in our sailing, as did Peter Stockton when he visited us. To sail out of Stonington Harbor into Fisher's Island Sound with the sloop keeling to the wind, with the water lapping over the lee gunwale, gliding through the waters, feeling the throb of the tiller as we careened along, was a real joy. Sailing, handling the boat, keeping it clean and in good shape, helped to build the foundations of self-confidence and commitment to life.

As I approached puberty I had twice suffered mastoiditis, which required two mastoid operations and also involved sinus infections. This led my parents, in my senior year, to enroll me in the Evans School on the Arizona desert south of Tucson. My year at the Evans School opened an entirely new vista in my young life. It was a boys' school and we were all in our mid-teens or later teenage years. The school campus consisted of a rectangle of screened cabins, each of which housed one of the school's students, as well as its instructors and classrooms. Adjacent to the campus was the school corral that housed the horses and mules. Each boy had his own horse, assigned to him by the school, and on weekends we were free to go camping in the Coronado Mountains that rose on the edge of the desert. We could take a pack mule, saddle our horse, and set off into the mountains.

To experience the desert, with the cacti blooming in spring, was, for an Easterner, born and raised in New York City, a transformative experience leading him into a new and unexplored world. The air, the sun, the warmth, the endless sky arching over the desert, lifted me out of myself and urged me on. It also served to clear up the tendency to infections.

But the year on the desert also brought its challenges. One day I returned from a trip, corralled my horse, and went to my cabin, noting as I went that the next-door cabin was packed with kids, crowding at the windows, who were all watching me intently. When I got to my cabin, I opened the door, and—"my God!"—there was a mule in my cabin! The watching crowd burst into hoots and hysterical laughter, but there was nothing for it; I had to haul the mule out of the cabin and lead her back to the corral, where she belonged, with the whole school reveling in my humiliation!

Looking back on this event, I came to realize that life wanted to wake me up, to shake me out of my phlegmatic, self-satisfied self to face the world—and become a "man."

But it was also during these years that my brother Edward suffered a mild epileptic attack, which at that time was known as "petit mal." His treatment—which, fortunately, proved successful—involved a period of starvation which awoke the deepest sympathy in his older brother.

Although, as already mentioned, starting in seventh grade, I found myself a year ahead of Peter in school, our friendship continued and we shared each other's lives. Boulderwood became for Peter a second home where he spent many vacations and greatly enjoyed taking part in the life of the farm.

At one point during our boyhood days, our mother engaged the help of a gifted Russian émigré, Mr. Melchior, an architect and designer, to remodel and decorate the interior of our house. In order to get the boys out of the way, Mother acquired a screened cabin which was set up on the lawn, under the trees, and became our "summer dormitory" with room for our friends to join us on the farm. We thought this was a great idea and we thoroughly enjoyed our life in the new "dormitory."

I remember especially one occasion when I was ten or eleven years old when Peter and a couple of other friends visited during the summer vacation. We discovered a pit that had been dug near the path behind the barn leading down the lane toward the blackberry patch. The pit was about three feet square and perhaps four or five feet deep and was out of sight. We invented what might have been known as a "pee-ing party" where we boys would stand around the pit and pee in an arching curve creating a kind of human "fountain." We decided that this should be described in a book entitled: "The Golden Stream" by I. P. Freely, its distinguished author.

The Stockton family also provided a kind of second home to me which enabled me to share in the cultural activities in which they were actively engaged. One, in particular, opened a door into a world with which I, otherwise, had no connection. This was the world of the theater. America's entry into the First World War had, amongst other things, opened a window to a wider world of human and cultural experience. And one of the ways in which this affected life in this country, especially in New York City, was an initiative to introduce the Moscow Art Theater which brought creative individuals like Richard Boleslavsky and Michael Chekhov to this country. This led to the establishment of the American Laboratory Theater in which Peter's parents, Herbert and Miriam Stockton, were actively engaged. It was an awakening experience to be invited by the Stocktons to attend an occasional off-Broadway performance, as well as dress rehearsals of productions by the Laboratory Theater.

As my college years approached, I decided to desert Yale, to which it was taken for granted in the Barnes family every self-respecting young man would go. I enrolled as a freshman at Harvard in 1929 in order to share the college years with Peter who was committed to attending Harvard the following year.

It was in those years that Harvard, under the leadership of President Eliot, was establishing its new dormitories on the Charles River, but the college also wanted every Harvard graduate to experience one year in the Harvard Yard. As a result, Freshman Year was to be spent in the Yard before moving down to the new houses. Thus it was in my third year and Peter's second that we were able to room together in Dunster House on the river.

Meanwhile, in my freshman year I had met a classmate whose family knew the Stocktons in New York City. And in our sophomore year, John and I decided to room together, although I had already told John that Peter and I intended to room together the following year. As it turned out, my year as John's roommate had an unexpected effect on me, which I mention because it may have, in some way, played into the tragedy destined to occur a year later.

As John's roommate, I began to observe that John's presence had a strange effect on me. It was as though I "froze up" in some mysterious way when we were together. This was not because of anything John did or said; it simply happened. But, in spite of this, as our year together came to an end, I didn't want to hurt John's feelings and suggested he might like to take a room near us so that we could stay in touch. So, in this way, it came about that John was a neighbor when Peter and I roomed together the following year. And during this year I still noticed this odd freezing up when we happened to be together. Peter and I never discussed this experience, and I have no idea whether it affected Peter in any way. What I do know is that during the autumn when we were already rooming together, Peter made an appointment to speak with the Dean. Peter told me that the Dean had assured him that everything was in good shape; there was nothing for him to worry about, his grades were good, there seemed to be no problems. As I look back on our life together at this time, I realize how little awareness I had that Peter may have been experiencing questions and tensions leading toward the tragedy which was, evidently, destined to occur. But, having been born with a phlegmatic temperament, dramatic tensions were rarely, if ever, part of my life. However, in regard to what I have just related concerning my relationship with John, I later learned that he was undergoing psychiatric treatment and that his consultant had encouraged his relationship with Peter and me because he felt that it would be helpful to John.

As I look back on my years at Harvard, the experience that rises most happily and meaningfully, and still echoes in the heart of the old man, are the years of my participation as a member of the Harvard Glee Club under the dynamic and humorous leadership of Doc Davidson. In every one of these four years we were joined by the Radcliffe chorus which enabled us to tackle such majestic works as the Bach B-Minor Mass and the Brahms Requiem. And it was these two works which each became the focus of two of the four years, culminating in a performance in the spring in Boston's

Symphony Hall under the direction of Sergei Kousevitsky conducting the Boston Symphony Orchestra and accompanied by professional soloists.

This musical experience was a wonderful complement to my undergraduate major in the History and Literature of the 19th Century which included a number of outstanding courses that served to build the foundation of my later work as a teacher of history in Waldorf schools.

It was on a Friday in January 1932 that Peter left me a note saying that he would be away for the weekend. But he never returned. I had no idea where he had gone or what had become of him. A desperate search followed during which Peter's family hired detectives, but no traces could at first be found.

It was many days before Peter's family, the college authorities and I learned what had happened. We learned that Peter had gone to a part of the country with which—as far as we knew—he had no previous connection. He went first to Detroit, where he bought a gun, then traveled up the Michigan peninsula to a town called Bad Axe, and there took another bus to a village called Harbor Beach on the shore of Lake Huron. There he took a room in a village inn where he kneeled down beside his bed, and with Bacon's essay on death open on the bed in front of him, shot himself through the heart.

On entering the inn, Peter had registered as Peter Barrow and had given Santa Fe, New Mexico as his home. The population of Harbor Beach was largely made up of Scandinavian immigrants, and when they found Peter's body they were, at first, convinced that this young man came from the East, rather than from the West, and they felt sure that his people would find him. But as days passed, and no one showed up, they finally decided that Santa Fe must be notified. They had, meanwhile, cared for Peter's body and had lit candles in the more traditional European way.

Peter's older sister, Anne Stockton Goodwin, was living with her husband and two small boys in Santa Fe, and it was her husband, Sage Goodwin, who saw a photograph in a Santa Fe paper and recognized Peter on his deathbed.

Peter's body was returned to his family in New York City, and it was there that his funeral service was held in the chapel of Grace Church.

After Peter's death we also learned that he had taken two other books with him besides Bacon's Essays: *Only Yesterday* by Frederick Lewis Allen and the *Meditations of Marcus Aurelius* in which he had underlined a number of passages including: "I must be true to myself as the emerald is true to its greenness." *Only Yesterday* is a brilliant journalistic review of the 1920s characterizing the rampant materialism of those post-war years.

But into this tragedy a mystery was inscribed. His mother, Miriam Stockton, while she was pregnant with Peter, had read a book by a man called Rudolf Steiner. The book was entitled

Peter Stockton

Knowledge of Higher Worlds and Its Attainment. The book impressed Mrs. Stockton deeply, but with Peter's birth and her own busy life, she put the book aside and went on with her life. However, with the tragedy of Peter's disappearance and death she remembered this book, although she still knew nothing further about its author. In the weeks following Peter's death, his father, Herbert Stockton, saw an announcement in *The New York Times* in which Rudolf Steiner's name was mentioned and, with this, Mrs. Stockton was able to come into contact with individuals in New York City who were students of Rudolf Steiner. And it was from these people that she learned that a conference was planned for the summer of 1933 for the purpose of introducing Steiner's work in this country. This conference was to be held in the township of Spring Valley in Rockland County, New York where a community actively engaged with Steiner's work, known as Threefold Farm, had been established in 1926. And it was to this conference that Peter's sister and I were invited by Mrs. Stockton in July 1933. Thus my friendship with Peter led me to what was to become the central calling of my life.

Ralph Courtney was the leader of the Threefold Group which hosted the conference. Ralph was born in America but had grown up in England and became an international journalist stationed in Paris following the end of the First World War. He had encountered the work of Rudolf Steiner and had come to know him personally. He visited Dornach, Switzerland, where Steiner's work was centered, and it was Steiner who asked whether he would be willing to return to the land of his birth in order to bring his work, known as Anthroposophy, to the attention of the American public. Reluctant at first, Courtney eventually agreed, and, in May 1921, left for New York City. There he contacted the small circle of individuals interested in Steiner's work, and it was largely Courtney's initiative that led to the formation of The Threefold Group and the establishment of the Threefold Vegetarian Restaurant on West 56th Street. It was also Ralph Courtney who realized how much it might mean if a center could be established for Steiner's work in an area within easy access of the city, but in a country situation with room to expand. This led to the purchase of the land in Spring Valley and to the first conference in North America to introduce Steiner's anthroposophy, also known as spiritual science, in July 1933.

The initiative to purchase the property in Spring Valley and to establish the Threefold Community was made financially possible by Charlotte Parker, a well-to-do lady who had originally come down from Boston to study art in New York City and had there met Steiner's work and had become an important source for the financial support of the Threefold initiative both in the city, and later in Spring Valley.

Courtney, with Charlotte Parker's support, had invited three speakers from Europe to introduce Steiner's work at this first anthroposophical conference. Two of the three speakers—Maria Roeschl and Ernst Lehrs, were teachers in the original Waldorf School in Stuttgart, Germany, founded by Rudolf Steiner in 1919 at the urgent request of Emil Molt, owner-director of the Waldorf-Astoria Cigarette factory from which the school received its name. The third speaker was a young scientist by the name of Ehrenfried Pfeiffer, destined to play an important part in the introduction and development of Steiner's work in America.

Thus it was that in July 1933, shortly before my 21st birthday, having just graduated from Harvard College, I was a member of an audience of some 30 or 40 people in a large open tent, at the edge of a wood, just below a low wooden structure known as the Summer Kitchen. And it was on the porch of this building that I found myself as a young man in the company of a group of ladies of various ages weaving our way around the tables, in a form of movement called Eurythmy. With hindsight I realize that this was the challenge imposed by destiny to test my courage and determination to pursue this new path.

What especially impressed me in what the three speakers presented was everything that Maria Roeschl and Ernst Lehrs told about the school in which they were both teachers. As already mentioned, Peter and I were both Lincoln School students from first grade through high school, and, following Peter's death, I had begun to wonder what role our education might have played in Peter's tragedy. For Peter was not the only gifted Lincoln student to take his own life. As I wrestled with this question I came to realize that the educational ideal on which the school and its philosophy were based was the concept of self-expression. Whatever a student undertook, if it truly expressed his or her inmost, creative self, was valid. But the years during which Peter and I grew up were the post-war years of intensifying materialism. They were the Prohibition years of bootlegging and the speakeasy. And they were the years in which the U.S. was discovering its potential wealth and power. When Peter and I graduated from high school we soon learned that the world was not buying a value just because it expressed one's innermost self. As a result, the more I pondered these matters, the more the question arose in me: Is there an education that could help to ground its students more firmly in their whole humanity? And it was especially what Roeschl and Lehrs shared about the education that underlay the ideals of Waldorf schooling which convinced me that here was such an education truly grounded in the reality of human development. As this conviction deepened, the determination awoke and grew: I want to go to Stuttgart and learn about this school and this education!

Prior to Peter's death, teaching as a career had been far from my thoughts. I wanted to do something *important*! Foreign service, in some form, seemed an attractive direction. But, with Peter's passing, teaching seemed to become more and more a real calling.

Almost immediately after the conference ended I turned twenty-one and inherited a thousand dollars! But I already had a good job for the coming year; I was engaged to be trained as an assistant to the headmaster of the Choate School in Wallingford, Connecticut—a prestigious boys' boarding school. So, I realized that it was only fair for me to inform Mr. St. John, the headmaster, that I intended to leave for Europe when my year of training ended. With this in mind, I went to Wallingford to inform Mr. St. John of my intention, and his response was a smile and the observation: "Why don't you go now and get it out of your system. And then come back to Choate!"

I was free! But there was another factor. During the conference, as I heard about the school in Stuttgart, I thought of Edward, my next younger brother, who was going through an adolescent crisis at Andover, the boarding school he attended. And I realized what this Waldorf school might also mean to him. I consulted Mrs. Stockton and she agreed that we invite him to come to Spring Valley to hear about this school. And so we did, and Edward came. It only needed a very short time before Edward announced: "That's the school I want to go to!"

But what would our family say to this radical idea? We invited Dr. Roeschl and Dr. Lehrs to visit us in Stonington on their way back to Europe, to which they agreed. When Edward and I announced the possibility that he might join me in the voyage to Stuttgart, our father was alarmed and hesitant, but our mother—always the pioneer—said: "If Henry goes, Edward should go too!" And so it came about that the sixteen-year-old and the newly-turned twenty-one-year-old found themselves as passengers with Roeschl and Lehrs on their way to Cuxhaven, the port of Hamburg, where they landed in late August. We were welcomed by a little lady with bright blue eyes behind steel-rimmed glasses to whom we were introduced as Fräulein Dr. Caroline von Heydebrand, a colleague who planned to drive south to Stuttgart with us.

As we drove through Hamburg, we passed the beautiful Alster lake. A fresh breeze was blowing and the lake was alive with white-crested waves. The two young Americans yearned to get out on the lake and sail. To our surprise the little lady who had met us volunteered to come along. Soon we were out on the lake, the sails billowing and the boat keeling to the wind. Our passenger glanced apprehensively at the waves dashing past the lee gunwale as the boat careened along in the stiff breeze. Fortunately we didn't capsize, but returned Caroline von Heydebrand safely to shore. Little did we realize at the time that she was one of the most distinguished members of the original Waldorf School faculty.

Having arrived in Stuttgart, I entered the teacher training program. But this was early September 1933 and Adolf Hitler had been elected Chancellor of Germany on January 30th of that same year. Following his election, the Parliament building—the Reichstag—was set on fire and burned to the ground and immediately thereafter Hitler demanded that he be given absolute authority to "save Germany from the Communists." Parliament agreed to his demand and, starting in February/March, Hitler and the National-Socialist Party that he controlled were given unlimited power.

As a student I experienced the Waldorf School being gradually strangled by the Hitler government. Jewish teachers were forced to leave. Every lesson was to begin with "Heil Hitler." The school was forbidden to take on a new first grade. Parents who refused to send their children to the Hitler Youth experienced difficulties of one kind or another. And, on March 30, 1938, the Waldorf School was finally closed by order of the Nazi government.

But, in addition to these outer attacks, I also came to realize that the faculty was being riven by internal tensions. Following Rudolf Steiner's death on March 30, 1925, divisions had gradually intensified within the Anthroposophical Society. Ita Wegman, MD, and Elisabeth Vreede, PhD, both members of the original Leadership Council (Vorstand) appointed by Rudolf Steiner at the Christmas Foundation Meeting in 1923, found themselves opposed by the Society leadership with which Marie Steiner— Rudolf Steiner's widow—was identified. These difficulties intensified and culminated at the Annual General Meeting of the Society's membership at the Goetheanum in Dornach in 1935 with the exclusion of Wegman and Vreede from the Vorstand. Their exclusion led to the withdrawal of the British and Dutch Societies in the ensuing years. Already in 1934 I found these tensions within the Anthroposophical Society so deeply disturbing that in the early summer I got on my bicycle in Stuttgart and rode through the Black Forest to Dornach (Switzerland), where the Goetheanum was located, in the hope of coming to an understanding of what was going on. On the way, I spent the night in a youth hostel where I was taken for a Russian. I soon realized that this was due to the handsome embroidered smock I was wearing, which I had sewn myself as part of my Waldorf training. On arrival at the Goetheanum, the first person I met was an American woman by the name of Arvia MacKaye who agreed to help me obtain interviews with the five individuals who comprised the Leadership Council, or Vorstand. It should here be noted that Arvia MacKaye was later destined to be my sister-in-law and a significant colleague in the evolution of Rudolf Steiner's work in North America.

I first met with Marie Steiner in Villa Hansi, which had been her home with Rudolf Steiner. Not a word was mentioned by Frau Dr. Steiner in reference to the difficulties within the Vorstand and the Society. She talked with me about Eugene O'Neil and American drama. Albert Steffen, appointed by Rudolf Steiner as the Society's vice-president, met with me in his apartment, but, again, no word about the internal difficulties in the Society's leadership. Steffen talked with me about Walt Whitman. Dr. Günther Wachsmuth, the Society's young, capable treasurer, had little time to waste with this foolish young American, and it was only in my meetings with Frau Dr. Wegman and Dr. Elisabeth Vreede that I glimpsed the tragedy that eventually led to their expulsion from the Leadership Council.

In this way I tried to get to the bottom of the difficulties threatening to divide the Society. Following my visit I left Dornach and spent the night on the island of Reichenau in the Lake of Constance. The island was known for its three churches dating from the early Middle Ages and, standing in one of the churchyards, I realized that it would be years before I could really understand the difficulties threatening to divide the Society. However, I was grateful to have had the opportunity to meet the five members of the original Vorstand even though I could only hope that understanding would eventually arise. An unexpected consequence occurred from my visit with Dr. Wegman. My attention was drawn to an institution for the care and education of children and young people with mental and physical disabilities, affiliated with the clinic under Dr. Wegman's direction. It occurred to me that the opportunity to gain practical experience of such work with the handicapped could be a valuable contribution to my future work as a Waldorf teacher to which I was fully committed. Dr. Wegman encouraged me in this regard and assured me that the Sonnenhof was in need of coworkers and that I would be welcome to participate after finishing my year in Stuttgart. I also learned that all four of Steiner's Mystery Dramas were scheduled for production in the coming summer at the Goetheanum, and this was an opportunity I did not want to miss. As a result, the summer of 1934 found me at the Goetheanum, following which I joined the Sonnenhof as a coworker. Both experiences proved to be invaluable contributions to the work I was to undertake when I finally returned home to America. Though my six months at the Sonnenhof were strenuous, they were an invaluable preparation for my career as a Waldorf teacher.

It was during my time at the Sonnenhof that I came to know a fellow American coworker, Gladys Barnett (later Gladys Hahn), as well as Drake Hale, the developmentally handicapped son of Roger and Marion Hale, whom I later came to know as colleagues and friends in the anthroposophical movement in America. Gladys Hahn played a key role in introducing the work with the handicapped and retarded in this country and was instrumental in the establishment of the Camphill Movement in America.

On my way home to the U.S. I was invited to teach a block of history to the eleventh grade in the recently established first Waldorf school in the English-speaking world, known as the New School, located in Streatham Hill in South London. The New School later rechristened itself as Michael Hall, now located in Forest Row, Sussex. Arriving in

With my First Grade at the New School

England, I found myself as the history teacher for a lively, and charming group of students, amongst whom were two young women, one destined to be the wife of Francis Edmunds, who later founded Emerson College, and the other to be the wife of Karl Nunhöfer, MD, one of the first doctors to practice anthroposophically extended medicine in England. These lively young people soon realized that their history teacher was only a few years older than they were, and they *enjoyed themselves*! However, Cecil Harwood and other colleagues had the courage to invite me to be the class teacher for the first grade starting its elementary school career the following autumn. I agreed, with the understanding that I could not promise to carry the class for the full eight years. This was accepted, and I soon found myself teaching my twenty-four first graders, now—as I write this—distinguished men and women in their late seventies. After the outbreak of war in 1940, one of them, Frederick Moyer, was sent to New York City by his mother to finish his schooling under my guardianship.

The four years which followed proved to be not only years of intensifying world destiny leading to the outbreak of World War Two but also

As Circus Director at the New School

foundation-building years in the biography of the young teacher at the New School/Michael Hall. I look back with gratitude to these years of broadening and deepening experience with colleagues like Francis Edmunds, Cecil Harwood, Jesse Darrell, Captain Field and many others. I was privileged to be asked to stand in for Francis Edmunds in the leadership of a summer camp on the Sussex coast which then led—in my fourth year and final summer—to finding myself as the leader of a large international camp on the coast of Wales in July/August 1939. We were a group of about a hundred young teenage campers from twelve or thirteen different countries. The camp was situated on the shore of Caernarvon Bay, looking westward across St. George's Channel and the Irish Sea toward Ireland. We gathered each evening—after lively, active days—in a great circle in which one of our national groups would sing a song from their native culture, and we then all joined together to sing our camp song "In the Quest of the Holy Grail" with words by Michael Wilson to music by Sibelius. On several such occasions, an echo floated back to us from the Welsh village situated not far away in the rolling Caernarvon hills as a village chorus responded with a Welsh folksong.

At the camp in Wales

As we know, the war began on September 3 with the invasion of Poland by the German army under Hitler's command, and I was moved to learn that a senior camper from a Waldorf school in Germany had flown over the campsite of the previous summer on a reconnaissance flight for the German Luftwaffe.

It was also during these years that I was blessed to have been granted an experience which has remained with me through all the many, many years that have since ensued. I include it here as a treasured memory along with the painting that conveys something of the magic of the experience I describe.

It was spring 1937 or, possibly, 1938. I had been invited by Cecil Harwood and Francis Edmunds to spend Easter with them in Cornwall on the west coast of England, near Tintagel and King Arthur's Castle. It had been a beautiful vacation. We were now on our way home to Streatham Hill in South London, where we were busy teaching at The New School.

A lively, friendly rain shower had come up behind us and had overtaken us as we entered Salisbury Plain on our way eastward toward London. Cecil's old Dodge was no racing car, and the shower glided past us as we approached Stonehenge. It was afternoon and the sun was descending in the western sky.

In those days, Stonehenge was not fenced and one had direct access from the road. We parked just off the road and walked up to the ancient Druidic circle. The air around the stones was filled with moisture as the shower had just passed by. As we approached, a beautiful rainbow arched directly over the circle, so close that we could see the green grass behind

Stonehenge by William Trost Richards (American 1833-1905)

it through the rainbow's end. And as we stood in awe, the full moon rose, directly above and behind the stones, within the rainbow's arch. And there we were: the sun setting in the west behind us, with the full moon within the rainbow above the stones welcoming us to Stonehenge!

But the central blessing in the biography of the young man that is recounted here was that destiny allowed me to meet the younger sister of Arvia MacKaye who had helped me to obtain the interviews with the five members of the Society's original Vorstand. Christy MacKaye and I met at the Goetheanum in the summer of 1936, at which time Christy was a pupil of Marie Steiner in the art of speech formation. But in the tensions which were threatening to divide the Anthroposophical Society this meeting was also a dramatic karmic challenge. As already mentioned, I had encountered the threatening divisions within the faculty of the Stuttgart Waldorf School, and they had moved me to mount my bicycle and ride through the Black Forest to Dornach to try to understand what

With Christy on the terrace of the Goetheanum, Easter 1939

was going on. So here was I, closely affiliated with Dr. Ita Wegman, heart-smitten with love for a pupil of Marie Steiner. And it was just these two individuals around whom the tensions wove which threatened to split the Society. This was, nevertheless, a fact of life that could not be avoided. In consequence, the young lovers studied Steiner's *Occult Movements of the 19th Century* in a determined effort to try to understand what threatened to separate them. And love triumphed! On September 5, 1939—two days after the outbreak of the war—we were united in marriage in what was then the Dornach home of Percy MacKaye, Christy's father, with Albert Steffen, Percy's poet friend, as part of the festive gathering.

The newlyweds then found themselves at home in Dornach in the northwest corner of Switzerland during the first year of the war. Christy's mother, Marion Morse MacKaye, had passed away on June 1 in St. Germain-en-Laye, just outside of Paris, where she and Percy MacKaye had gone to visit a friend, Gordon Craig. Following Marion's death, Percy had returned to Dornach to be with Arvia and Christy and

After the wedding

with the many friends who cherished and supported him, amongst them especially his poet-friend Albert Steffen. The months that followed Marion MacKaye's death evoked an outpouring of poetic expression in her loving, widowed husband that culminated in his volume, *My Lady Dear, Arise*, first published in Switzerland by Emil Birkhäuser & Cie., Basel, 1940, and later by Macmillan in the United States.

With the outbreak of war on September 3, 1939, the Barnes/MacKaye family found itself in the protected independence of neutral Switzerland. Christy and Arvia's older brother Robin, who had suffered a breakdown, was at this time also in Europe in the care of Sanatorium Wiesneck in southern Germany in the neighborhood of Freiburg.

With the outbreak of war, Robin could not remain in Germany, and he joined his father and sister in Dornach. Curiously, my younger brother Alfred had also found his way—quite unexpectedly—to Europe shortly before the war began. Alfred was a student at Exeter Academy where he lightheartedly engaged in a rapier duel which led to his expulsion from the Academy. This occurred while our parents were visiting Edward and me in Europe, so there was nothing for it, except that Alfred must join us, and, in this way, he also found himself as a student in the Waldorf School in Stuttgart, where he completed his high school education. Alfred undertook to care for Robin in Dornach where we all spent the first year of the war.

Although Switzerland was neutral and not directly involved in the war, the northwest corner of Switzerland—looking directly north across the Rhine to the Black Forest of Southern Germany and west across the open fields of Eastern France to the Vosges Mountains—was a highly dramatic situation from which to experience the course of the war.

The Maginot Line—the French fortifications along the Rhine—extended from Basel, where the Rhine turned north, creating the border between France and Germany up to Belgium. It was self-evident that Hitler's army would either attempt to circumvent these defenses by breaking through Belgium, to the north, or by cutting through the corner of Switzerland at Basel, to the south. This threat hung like the sword of Damocles over the northwest corner of Switzerland until the die was cast and the German army invaded Belgium and forced its way into France from the north. This finally occurred on the 7th of May, 1940, due, in part, to pressure by Mussolini, Hitler's Italian ally, who urged him to take this northern route. Meanwhile, rumors of the threatened invasion of France via Basel kept the tension in the northwestern corner of Switzerland at an intensely high level, causing the Swiss government to issue an order for the evacuation of this potentially vulnerable area by those who could find shelter in the Swiss mountains. Swiss soldiers occupied the Goetheanum, and Percy MacKaye, Arvia, Alfred Barnes and Robin all took refuge in Montreux, overlooking the Lake of Geneva. Christy and I, however, decided to stay and have our honeymoon in Dornach despite the risks.

The last American ship to leave the Mediterranean was scheduled to depart from Genoa on June 1. At the very end of May, Christy and I said farewell to our friends in Dornach who had decided not to leave, and we joined the family in Montreux. On our way, Christy was able to receive her diploma in *Sprachgestaltung* (Speech Formation) from Marie Steiner in Beatenberg where she had taken refuge when Dornach was evacuated. Having rejoined our family in Montreux, we waited until the last day of May—to avoid the risk of being trapped in Italy if she declared war before we sailed—and arrived in Genoa on the 31st just as the S.S. Manhattan pulled into port. The hotel where we spent that night was crowded with Japanese, now part of the Axis of Germany, Italy and Japan. It was, therefore, on June 1—a year, to the day, since Christy's mother had passed away in Saint-Germain-en-Laye—that we embarked on a vessel packed to the brim with refugees from many different nations, desperate to escape the tragedy that had, once again, descended on Europe and was in the process of engulfing the world. We sailed safely westward, crossed the Strait of Gibraltar, and followed a southern route, hoping to avoid the threat of mines, and entered New York harbor on June 10, the day Italy declared war.

My Work Begins

Seven years! The young man who landed in New York on June 10, 1940, was a very different young man from the youngster who set sail for Europe in August 1933. How was he different? What had I learned?

I was married... had found a wonderful life companion. I had a profession, was a teacher, and was truly grateful to be one. I felt a destiny connection with the children—the young human beings—whose teacher I had been from first through fourth grade. Europe, including England, had been my home during these seven years, from the time I came of age until I was twenty-eight. I had met the work of Rudolf Steiner and knew that this was my life's true path. I had joined the community of the Anthroposophical Society and had made the further commitment of membership in the esoteric School of Spiritual Science. Each of these steps had proven to be in inner agreement with my whole life's direction.

We were met at the dock in New York by Percy's brother, Benton MacKaye, forester, father of the Appalachian Trail, and co-founder of the Wilderness Society, who welcomed us heartily on our return to our native land. His welcome was seconded by my parents—Henry and Mabel Barnes—who invited us to the farm in Stonington, Connecticut, to gather our wits and plan for the future.

It soon became clear that I was needed at the Rudolf Steiner School in New York City for the coming school year. The Steiner School had been founded in 1928 as the first Waldorf school in America and was, at this time, located at 20 West 73rd Street, just half a block west of Central Park. The school's enrollment hovered between sixty and seventy students and was limited to kindergarten and the elementary grades. It was, however, just at this time that the Waldorf educational movement was beginning to take root and grow. The Kimberton Waldorf School opened its doors in 1941 in Pennsylvania and was followed a year later by High Mowing in Wilton, New Hampshire, a day and boarding high school.

Back in New York

In my first year (1940/41) I taught a combined third and fourth grade. But as the school year ended, the school lost its lease on the 73rd Street building. Mercifully, we discovered a building for lease at 49 East 91st Street to which the school emigrated in the summer of 1941. Quaintly enough, 91st Street between Park and Lexington Avenues had been home to the writer of this tale for many years. And here I was, teaching my fifth grade on the very block where I had played catch back and forth across the street in my boyhood years.

But these were war years. Pearl Harbor, December 7, 1941, catapulted the U.S. into World War Two, and in the spring of 1943 the young Waldorf teacher was drafted into the army. I still remember the look of puzzled surprise on the face of the officer who was drafting me as he studied the records and observed that this draftee was a Harvard graduate whose annual salary at that time was $1150! Despite the Harvard degree, the new recruit did not apply for OTS (Officers Training School) because I felt unable to assume that degree of individual responsibility in the complex circumstances which had led to the war.

On June 27, 1943, in a Jewish hospital in Harlem where a natural birth was still possible, my son John Michael Barnes entered the dramatic destiny of the 20th Century.

I had assumed, because of my years of European experience, that I would be sent to Europe, but the army shipped me to Puerto Rico to teach Puerto Rican troops the ideals of American democracy. For this purpose we were provided with a text, featuring Private Pete, to demonstrate these ideals. As we guided our trainees through Private Pete, we could look

out the window and observe those
we had guided being lined up in
preparation for shipment to Texas for
basic training: all the lighter-skinned,
straight-haired men in one line, and
the darker-skinned, kinky-haired in
another. Certainly, this was an odd
way for the U.S. Army to live out the
democratic ideals we were training
our troops to defend.

As I was spared front-line
combat and had personal contacts in
Puerto Rico, it became possible for
Christy and Johnny Michael to join
me, and we were happily reunited.
As the war ended, we returned to
New York where I received my

With my two children

discharge early in '46 and was able to apply my service benefit to enroll
in Teachers College where I received my MA in the teaching of history
before returning to the Steiner School the following year.

It was during the war years that the Rudolf Steiner School was
finally able to acquire its own permanent home at 15 East 79th Street.
Three years after the school had moved into the rented building on East
91st Street this building was sold and the school, in the late summer of
1944, was homeless. Rental properties during the war were prohibitively
expensive, but, here and there, an unoccupied mansion was available for
the, then, formidable sum of $50,000! Fortunately, by that time the Steiner
School included sturdy young students and a committed community of
parents who rallied to the cause and decided to issue bonds and buy the
building. In this way, the Rudolf Steiner School, now sixteen years of
age, found its permanent home in a beautiful, spacious building on a wide
cross-town street within half a block of Central Park and the Metropolitan
Museum of Art.

It was to this fortunate situation that the young warrior returned in the autumn of 1946, unscathed except for his somewhat naïve democratic idealism.

A year later, our daughter Marion was born in a Catholic hospital on East 86th Street in Manhattan, and with her arrival our family was complete.

With the exception of my three years in the army, the thirty-seven years from 1940 until my retirement in 1977 were grounded in my life as a member of the faculty of the Rudolf Steiner School. These years witnessed the growth of the school from an elementary school whose enrollment hovered between sixty and seventy children in a rented school building on the city's West Side to a full twelve-year school with two thriving kindergartens and an enrollment of nearly three hundred students, housed in two substantial buildings owned by the school, within half a block of Central Park and the Metropolitan Museum of Art. To have been privileged to be a member of the Rudolf Steiner School faculty during these years was a source of inner strength for which I am truly grateful. To have had colleagues such as Amos Franceschelli, Dorothy and William Harrer, Virginia Paulsen, Margaret DeRis, Lona Koch, Nanette Grimm, Kari van Oordt, Thorn Zay, Karl and Arvia Ege, to name only a few, was to know oneself to be part of a truly human and truly professional community. I was astonished recently to discover that I was annually elected Faculty Chairman for twenty-eight of those years, from 1946 to 1974. Looking back on these years, I now ask myself why I was asked, year after year, to continue as the faculty's chairman. As I remember, it was never that I sought the office. In fact, I recall that on a number of occasions when the faculty was about to elect its chairman for the coming year, I left the meeting in order to eliminate any embarrassment on the part of my colleagues if they wanted to bring about a change of leadership. And, as I try to understand what was the underlying reason that the faculty wanted me to continue as chairman, I have come to realize that it may well have been my ability to maintain a human balance in a community that included a number of strong individualities amongst whom tensions could—and did—arise from time to time. In 1952, when our daughter Marion was five years old, Christy was able to join the faculty, first

Teaching at the Rudolf Steiner School

as a class teacher, which Teddy Wilson, one of Christy's cherished children, described as "combat training," and was then finally freed to become—what destiny truly intended her to be—a wonderful high school teacher of English and literature.

But in these years—the early 1950s—there was no high school and the increased enrollment we had hoped for failed to materialize. As their children approached the 8th grade, many parents, in order to assure their children of a high school education in schools that provided a secure entry to the college years, withdrew their children in the 7th and even as early as the 6th grade. In consequence, enrollment remained static and the school's financial situation continued to be precarious. It was not only these more outward circumstances, however, that awoke the realization in the minds and hearts, especially of the more experienced teachers: we need a high school! We need to accompany these young people through their adolescent years into early adulthood if the education of their early years is truly to be the ground for their later lives. And this growing conviction was strongly supported by the presence of an experienced teacher who had recently joined the faculty. Karl Ege was one of the very last teachers in the original Waldorf School in Stuttgart, Germany, to have been personally appointed to the College of Teachers by Rudolf Steiner. And he had agreed to join our faculty not only to strengthen the educational life of the New York school, but to provide guidance and experience in the furthering of the Waldorf movement as a whole, still in its pioneering phase in North America. And it was clear to Karl Ege, as well as to other experienced European colleagues like Francis Edmunds, who strongly encouraged and supported the growth of Waldorf education in this country, that the Steiner School needed to become a full twelve-year school. It was already clear, at this time, that the faculty included a number of teachers who could pioneer the high school: Amos Franceschelli would be a wonderful teacher of math and physics; Nanette Grimm of biology and chemistry; Christy MacKaye Barnes of English, drama, and speech; and her husband, of history.

What class, what group of children, might spearhead the establishment of a high school? Virginia Paulsen's former class, which was guided through seventh and eighth grades by Karl Ege and Christiane Sorge, had the vitality, the ability, and the commitment to pioneer the venture.

But a full high school could not be housed in the 79th Street building; a new building would be required. The school was in its 20th year and enjoyed the support of a strong body of parents, former parents, alumni and friends amongst whom Beatrice Straight Cookson was prepared to lend crucially needed financial support. But where was the building the high school would need, even though a ninth grade could still be housed in the elementary school building? This was the final challenge.

It was spring, 1955. Virginia Paulsen's former class, destined to be the graduating class of 1959, was in the 8th grade. And a former school building, exactly one block south of the 79th Street school, came on the market. What had been the Walt Whitman School at 15 East 78th Street was for sale! Destiny had spoken. The Board of Trustees, with Lawrence Smadbeck, its Treasurer, plunged in. The response was beyond all hopes and expectations, and, with Beatrice Cookson's central help, the necessary funds were raised.

I was teaching in a fourth-floor classroom when Katherine Reeve, the School's secretary, entered the room to tell me that Lawrence Smadbeck was on the phone. Negotiations for the purchase of the Walt Whitman School building had reached the decisive moment. He wanted to know whether the Steiner School was ready to buy the building. I interrupted the lesson and said to Katherine Reeve: "Yes, we'll go for it!" and the deed was done.

* * *

But both for Christy and myself, the recognition of the essential role of anthroposophy as the ground on which the education was based, grew steadily and deepened. I felt called to become a reader of the First Class of the School for Spiritual Science. It was a rare Friday, at the end of a busy week at school, that we failed to travel downtown to 211 Madison Avenue, between 35th and 36th Streets, to take part in the life of the Anthroposophical Society. Sometimes it was difficult to finish my work at school and get to 211 in time for an evening event. John G. Root, Sr., a former student and colleague of mine at the Rudolf Steiner School, recalls the following incident:

"The instance I have in mind, trivial yet characteristic, involves transportation under time pressure. On this occasion I offered to take Henry (at approximately 200 pounds) from the School on 79th Street to the Anthroposophical headquarters at 211 Madison Avenue behind me on the seat of my big Harley-Davidson motorcycle. I felt constrained to be very careful as we tooled down Park Avenue, navigating the tricky passage through the bowels of Grand Central Station, and parking right in front of our Society building, where, as I remember, Henry gave the lecture vividly and with no loss of aplomb. After a lively discussion period, Henry took the bus home."

Our family would never have survived had we not been able to leave the intense heat and noise of the city each summer and refresh ourselves at Christy's childhood home in Cornish, New Hampshire. Built on a high hillside by Christy's parents Percy and Marion MacKaye, this home became our summer refuge. Here, overlooking the Connecticut River valley to the west, we were able to drink in the peace and splendor of sunsets over the Green Mountains and spend the rest of our evenings reading aloud by kerosene lamplight. Part of each day was spent working in the garden or clearing the woods. This life was our link to nature and our pioneer forefathers—a source of inner and outer re-creation.

It was during these years that a remarkable opportunity developed in which we were grateful to be able to participate. Ernst and Marie Fetzer operated a thriving summer guest program on their biodynamic farm in New Hope, Pennsylvania, and in June—at the end of the school year— they offered the Steiner School faculty the opportunity to gather on their farm for anthroposophical study and a vacation at a price even a Waldorf teacher—in those days—could afford. Many faculty members and their families gladly availed themselves of this opportunity. The children helped in the kitchen and on the farm under Ernst and Marie's guidance, which was genuinely appreciated. It was also during these years that the school had initiated a week on a farm in Otis, Massachusetts in which the third grade—as part of its main lesson farming block—lived and worked on the small farm. The children looked back on this experience as one of the high points of their elementary school years. And it was as a result of this experience that the faculty came to realize what it would mean if the school were to have a working connection with a biodynamic farm directly related with the ideals which inspired the children's education. Meanwhile, the Fetzers—as well as the Pienings, another biodynamic farm family in upstate New York—found themselves confronted by a situation characteristic for many small family farmers. Their children had other plans for their lives than family farming, with the consequence that their parents were faced with the question: How are we to support ourselves in our old age when we are no longer able to maintain the farm? The Fetzers, for instance, saw no alternative except to sell the farm. Following the sale, they still lived nearby and had to observe their wonderfully fertile garden soil asphalted over for a parking lot.

This was just one individual instance of a situation confronting countless small American family farmers and, in this case, it led the Fetzers and the Pienings to realize what it would mean if they were part of an ongoing community that would provide long-range support for the farm activity. In this way—both from the side of the teachers who realized what it would mean if, over the years, the children could experience life and work on a practical farm, and from the side of the farmers who knew what it would mean if the farm were part of an ongoing community—a meeting emerged in October 1966 that led to the establishment of the Rudolf Steiner Educational and Farming Association, whose purpose was to achieve such a goal. The meeting was held in what had been Ehrenfried Pfeiffer's laboratory in the basement of the Threefold Auditorium in Spring Valley. Herbert Koepf, who at that time carried on Pfeiffer's agricultural initiatives, was also present on that occasion. Karl and Arvia Ege, both at that time teachers in the Rudolf Steiner School, were centrally involved in carrying out this initiative. Karl Ege reminded the gathering that when Steiner had been asked, in the discussion which followed his lectures in the agricultural course at Koberwitz in 1924, about the future of Germany, he had said that the cities of Germany would be in ruins and culture would be forced to withdraw to agricultural islands from which it would, once again, bring cultural life to spiritual rebirth, as it once had when the Celtic monks brought Christianity to the Germanic tribes in the early Middle Ages. It was also significant that, on this occasion, Arvia Ege, one of the five founding teachers of the Rudolf Steiner School in 1928, reminded those present that, if such a new initiative uniting education and agriculture were to be truly human and creative, the arts would also need to be represented.

With the establishment of the Association dedicated to the goal of helping to bring a farming community into existence in a close working relation with an existing urban Waldorf school seeking to incorporate farming experience into its curriculum, the search for the farm, for the money to buy it, and for the pioneers to get the initiative going could now begin. Life supported the venture. The Association saw in Thorn Zay, sculptor and teacher of woodworking, modeling and practical skills, the young man needed to get the search going, and Thorn accepted the challenge. Destiny provided the comrade needed to share in the search. Fentress Gardner, who had been an early farming apprentice under Ehrenfried Pfeiffer's direction, decided, in 1971, to retire early from the U.S. Foreign Service. He had played a crucial role in the aftermath of World War II, helping the Waldorf school in Stuttgart to reopen its doors, after having been closed by the Hitler government in 1938.

It had meanwhile become clear that Columbia County in upstate New York, south of Albany and adjacent to the Great Barrington area in western Massachusetts, would be a suitable location for the new enterprise. Camphill Village, Copake, NY, founded in 1961, had grown into a thriving community devoted to the care of the mentally and physically handicapped. The Village coworkers urgently wanted a Waldorf school for their children and were preparing to establish one in the Village. But when they learned of the possibility that such a school might come into existence within easy commuting range they were delighted because creating and sustaining such a school within the Village was not really practical. Arvia and Karl Ege had also recently retired to neighboring Hillsdale, NY and were both centrally engaged in support of the new venture. I was still teaching in New York City. With the general location now clearly determined, the search for a suitable property had found its focus. Nearly seventy farms were visited, many mapped and sketched by Arvia, who joined the search. And, in 1972, Thorn and Fentress returned to the Curtis Vincent farm in the township of Hillsdale and realized that—of all the farms visited—this was the best qualified from many points of view, and they urged the leadership of the Association to concentrate on its acquisition.

At this time I was in Europe recovering from a severe bout of pneumonia. Fentress reached me by phone while I was in Stuttgart staying with my son John's family at Haus Molt, the former residence of Emil Molt, the founder of the original Waldorf School. From Haus Molt I made a number of international phone calls with the fortunate result that three generous donors each pledged ten thousand dollars for the first three years. Consequently, the Rudolf Steiner Educational and Farming Association, on July 31, 1972, became the proud owner of what came to be known as Hawthorne Valley Farm, and the work began. Fentress bought day-old calves and gradually built up a herd of milking cows; Thorn Zay built double-decker bunks so that the Visiting Students Program could begin, and Jeanne Bergen, who had joined the initiative, started a biodynamic vegetable garden.

Camphill Village, however, announced that a school must begin that autumn or they would be forced to build a school in the Village, which they did not want to do. Those carrying the initiative for this new venture had assumed that they would have time to lay the foundations for the future community before launching the new school, but this was a luxury they were not to have. The school must begin that very autumn. Karl Ege went right to work, but, sadly, destiny did not grant him the opportunity to see the school into actual existence; he passed away before the school began. However, the school was meant to be. Rudolf Copple, an experienced and beloved teacher in the Rudolf Steiner School, was planning to retire that summer and was persuaded to "retire" to the hamlet of Harlemville in order to help launch the new initiative. Rudolf was joined by an energetic young teacher who was prepared to "cut his pedagogical teeth" on behalf of the new school, and James Pewtherer became a key player in the new venture, and later in the Waldorf movement as a whole.

After retiring from teaching at the Rudolf Steiner School, Christy and I decided to sell our brownstone house at 410 East 84ᵗʰ Street where we had been living for 25 years and move up to quiet Hillsdale, New York where we could be close to the growing Hawthorne Valley community in Harlemville. Arvia designed a little cottage for us on her property on Rodman Road. Leaving the city, which had been the center of our lives and work for so long, was a very big step for both of us.

After our move to Hillsdale it became possible for Christy and me to take a more active part in the development of the Harlemville initiative. I can remember the weekly Monday meetings at which all the co-workers of the organization came together: the farmers, the cooks and other staff of the Visiting Students Program, and the teachers at the Hawthorne Valley School. Much of the more important day-to-day management was discussed at these meetings: the purchase and sale of livestock and farm equipment, school events, enrollment and faculty, the scheduling of visiting classes in the Visiting Students Program, etc. As can be imagined, these meetings were sometimes tumultuous, and my experience as chairman of the faculty at the Rudolf Steiner School helped me navigate the stormy scenes that inevitably arose.

The Anthroposophical impulse was at the core of the Harlemville initiative, and soon there was a regular study group, the festivals were celebrated, Christy introduced the old English Shepherd's Play and started a speech chorus, and there were lectures as well as eurythmy and other artistic performances. Following a plan designed by Arvia, the large hayloft above the cow barn was converted into a performance space. The First Class of the School for Spiritual Science met on a monthly basis at Arvia's house in Hillsdale.

Chapter 45 in *Into the Heart's Land* provides an overview of the life and work which developed from the decision in October 1966 to create the Rudolf Steiner Educational and Farming Association. It is astonishing—especially to the old author of this autobiography—to realize the social, economic and cultural initiatives which have arisen from the decision forty-two years ago, to work toward such a goal. The Association now comprises many activities based on agriculture, education and the arts, in which approximately one hundred forty coworkers are directly engaged and which touch the lives of many hundreds of individuals in many different ways.

Before returning to the central autobiographical thread in this life story, I may be allowed to share an especially happy event which brought me back to Hawthorne Valley in the summer of 2006. It had been a special joy to be able to spend yet one more wonderful vacation at our summer home in New Hampshire. To be able, once again, to sit on the terrace, in front of the house, and look out to the west, across the Connecticut River Valley toward the distant Green Mountains of Vermont, with the majestic mass of Mount Ascutney toward the southwest in the nearer distance, was a gift of destiny for which I was profoundly grateful. And to have this gratitude compounded on the radiant afternoon of the twelfth of August, looking out toward the flower garden, behind the house, to find myself celebrating my ninety-fourth birthday by sharing in the joy of my grandson Benjamin Ober's marriage with Erika Argersinger was a crowning blessing.

A few days later to have been able to return to my present home in the Fellowship Community via Harlemville, where I found myself part of the annual General Meeting of the Biodynamic Farming and Gardening Association which had chosen Hawthorne Valley as the place to hold that year's meeting, was an unexpected pleasure. A huge tent had been set up on the school's campus between the school building and the stream, across which a sturdy wooden bridge, designed by one of the school's 10th graders, leads to the woods which enclose the valley to the east. Having been part of the gathering forty years before, when the decision was made to launch the Rudolf Steiner Educational and Farming Association, and now to find myself as part of the annual meeting of the Biodynamic Association—a national organization to carry forward this work in North America—was an unexpected, and happy, surprise, as well as a tribute to the farsighted, practical vision of Rudolf Steiner, the movement's founder.

Serving the Anthroposophical Society

Let me now turn to my work as a member of the Council of the Anthroposophical Society. An important experience for me was the initiative that led to the celebration of the centennial of Rudolf Steiner's birth in 1961, in which, as the Council's chairman, I was also personally involved.

The celebration of Rudolf Steiner's centennial was directly linked with the celebration of the 200th anniversary of Goethe's birth. It may well be surprising for Americans in the 21st century to realize how widely Goethe was acknowledged in this country in 1949, the 200th anniversary of his birth. This was especially true in California where August 28, Goethe's birthday, was officially declared "von Goethe Day" by the governor, and was the occasion of a significant celebration in San Francisco and the Bay area in which anthroposophists were actively engaged and Hans Pusch, Goetheanum speech artist and actor, played a special role.

Following the Goethe Bicentennial, the Society's Executive Council (Vorstand) at the Goetheanum responded enthusiastically to the invitation by the American Society for a Vorstand member to visit this country. Rudolf Grosse, at that time the newest member of the Vorstand, responded to the invitation, and in 1958 visited thirteen American cities. In the report of this visit, Grosse spoke of the "immeasurable inner enrichment that had flowed toward him." Grosse's visit proved to be a positive preparation for the celebration of Rudolf Steiner's Centennial three years later.

The Centennial was celebrated in many anthroposophical groups and found its central focus in the festival in New York City which was held at the Barbizon-Plaza Hotel, south of Central Park, on April 21, 1961. The Society's Council, working in close collaboration with the New York Branch, had realized how important it would be that the Centennial celebration be open to the public and that it should include the opportunity for visitors to experience an exhibition of Rudolf Steiner's life work. For this reason the Barbizon-Plaza was selected as a suitable location because it offered both a large auditorium and stage, as well as an excellent exhibition space in the mezzanine gallery easily accessible from the hall. The Society's building, 211 Madison Avenue, was inadequate for a public event of this kind.

During the night of April 20th, thanks to the heroic efforts of volunteers from the Rudolf Steiner High School, the mezzanine gallery was first cleared and then transformed into an exhibition space. The first section of the background was up by 2:00 a.m.; the second crew now went to work and covered the tables with blue burlap already cut and pre-fitted. Photographs and labels were now placed. By 6:00 a.m. the third crew arrived and gradually the three hundred volumes by Rudolf Steiner found their predestined place on the tables. This achievement was a remarkable example of the enthusiasm and disciplined organization of the Steiner school and its students. On Friday, April 21st the beautiful exhibit was well attended, and in the evening a large audience gathered in the hotel's auditorium. As the Council's chairman, I welcomed the audience and shared messages from Bruno Walter, the distinguished orchestral conductor who had become a devoted student of Rudolf Steiner's work, as well as from Albert Schweitzer. Olin Wannamaker, the Society's President, gave a short address which was followed by a talk by Rudolf Grosse, who had returned from Europe to renew his connection with the Society and the work in America. The evening concluded with an inspiring eurythmy performance starring Elena Zuccoli. This event, which I experienced as a high point in the life of the Anthroposophical Society, is described in more detail in *Into the Heart's Land*.

As we entered the 1970s, it became increasingly clear that the Anthroposophical Society in America needed to broaden its scope from being a primarily East-coast organization to one that was truly continental. It was especially members on the West Coast who were restive under what they perceived to be an East-coast domination, centered in New York City.

It was on the occasion of the Society's Annual General Meeting on April 22, 1978, that, in my situation as the Council's Chairman, I drew attention to the fact that during the preceding year (1977/78) the Council had met in Berkeley, California, in September, in Chicago in November and in New York in February. In this connection I pointed to the value of establishing personal contacts in these three major areas on the Society's behalf, but also to the difficulty, and cost, of doing so. It had become clearer, year by year, that there was a need for some form of regional cooperation. At that time, two meetings had already occurred in the Midwest. In consequence, when the national Council met in New York in February, it decided to meet only once during 1978-79 to provide the opportunity for each of the three then existing regions to explore the possibilities for more active regional collaboration. This, however, in no sense implied that there was no need for a national society.

The achievement of regionalization proved to be a three-year process which was concluded by a meeting of the newly inaugurated Council on February 20, 1981. The eight members of the new Council were: Dietrich Asten, Henry Barnes, Werner Glas, Sharon Keller, Traute Page, Carlo Pietzner, René Querido and Virginia Sease. All three of the major regions were represented in the new Council: René Querido and Virginia Sease from the West Coast, Traute Page, Werner Glas and Sharon Keller from the Midwest, and Dietrich Asten, Carlo Pietzner and Henry Barnes from the East Coast.

As a footnote to the regionalization process, it may be of interest to note that when the eastern interim regional Council was faced with the question of how best to select the one, two or three representatives to the new national Council, they chose a procedure which embodied not only a democratic element but also one which incorporated a more selective, spiritually oriented basis of judgment. Every member of the Society in the Eastern region received a letter in which he or she was invited to propose the name of individuals they felt were qualified to serve on such a Council. The names suggested would then be reviewed by the interim Council, responsible for making the final selection, which reserved the freedom to accept, reject, or modify the nominations received. The result was remarkable in that the three names most frequently suggested were also those whom the regional Council felt to be the best suited to meet the need. The three individuals most frequently suggested were: Dietrich Asten, Henry Barnes and Carlo Pietzner.

What I felt to be especially encouraging in this process of the Society's transformation was the way in which this came about. There was a positive recognition that the forms, and the procedures, should conform to the life and the needs of the organism rather than the other way around. It is who the individuals are, and how Anthroposophy lives in them that was recognized as essential.

As a member of the Council, I came to know and appreciate Dietrich Asten. He had emigrated to the United States in 1950 and played a decisive role in the development of Rudolf Steiner's work in this country until his death in 1984. He served as Chairman of the Council of the Anthroposophical Society from 1961 to 1973 and was president of the Board of Directors of the Anthroposophic Press from 1956 until his death. Dietrich and I were colleagues and friends during these years. When, for personal reasons, Dietrich decided in 1973 to resign as the Chairman of the Society's Council, I was elected to take his place.

A significant initiative occurred in 1981 in which I was directly involved and to which I look back with genuine appreciation. As the Society's General Secretary since 1974 it had been my responsibility to represent the American Society at the twice-yearly meetings of representatives of the worldwide General Anthroposophical Society at the Goetheanum. And it was to the meeting in October 1979 that I brought an invitation to the Executive Council (the Society's Vorstand) on behalf of both the societies in the United States and in Canada for a meeting of the Vorstand with members of the Society in North America in the spring of 1981. The suggestion was received with enthusiasm by the Goetheanum Vorstand and we went right to work.

I carried the message to our members in this country both directly in meetings with groups and branches, and through the printed word in our Newsletter. Rather than announcing an accomplished plan, the effort was always to invite and encourage initiative and participation. And the response of individuals like David Adams, active in the Section for the Visual Arts, Peter Menaker in the field of Speech and Drama, John Alexandra on behalf of the Threefold Community in Spring Valley, and many others, spoke of an awakening interest and genuine support.

It became clear that Threefold Farm in Spring Valley was ready to host such an event and had the resources and facilities to enable it to happen. Two elements emerged. One was the timing, as it became clear that late May 1981 was when it wanted to happen, which placed the event between Ascension and Whitsun, a time of inner testing and creative awakening. And what also became evident was the longing and the determination that the event itself should be creative, and have a truly artistic character. It was recognized that the innermost need of the Western World is to achieve a human balance between intellectual intelligence and will-driven energies that tend to dominate our Western culture today. As we prepared for the conference, we realized how much it would mean if we could find ways to address this threatening polarization of the human soul. And as we wrestled with these questions we saw, ever more clearly, that this required us to awaken to the need to nourish and strengthen the living presence of the human heart as the balance organ between the intellect and the will. As this insight deepened we realized that, for Rudolf Steiner, this had been the central impulse that had led him to refound the Anthroposophical Society at Christmas 1923. And it was in this way that the impulse of the Christmas Foundation was woven, as a central thread, into the conference and its preparation, together with the recognition that the conference itself must be a "work of art." Destiny, one might say, "heard the message," with the result that the conference, and the weeks that followed, became the dramatic climax of Peter Menaker's short, but most significant life.

Peter met Rudolf Steiner's work in his third year at college, and what interested and impressed him especially was Steiner's involvement with the dramatic arts. This led Peter to the Goetheanum in Dornach where he trained in the art of speech and drama. On his return to America he took up a work with Steiner's Mystery Dramas which had been inaugurated by Hans Pusch. Three years before his death, Peter was officially asked by the Society to lead this work. In consequence, he played a central role in the May conference in 1981. Each of the morning and evening plenum gatherings, with which each conference day began and ended, was introduced with a rhythmically repeated moment of eurythmy and a brief recitation by the speech chorus in which Peter participated. And it was largely thanks to Peter that we were able to experience the medieval scenes from Rudolf Steiner's Mystery Drama, *The Soul's Probation*, which Peter directed and in which he also acted.

To round out the picture of this remarkable event, one should be aware of the fact that it was announced by a beautiful, colorful, three-folded introductory leaflet which was received by every member in the United States and Canada. To bring this event to life for those who may be encountering this event for the first time, two paragraphs from the introductory leaflet will be included here.

"As the world situation in our time seems to grow ever more desperate and inhuman, anthroposophists can experience the urgent call for more vigorous and spiritually willed initiative. As western humanity, our pressing need is the energetic cultivation of that meditative 'balance of soul' most native to the middle sphere of life. It is a Michaelic clarity of heart that will fill in a fully human way the gap between spiritual and outer deed. …

One key to this work lies in the weaving rhythms and mantric forces of the Foundation Stone Meditation, which will stand behind all the endeavors of this conference. Together with the 1979 Michaelmas Active Members' Meeting in Dornach and other related events and ongoing work throughout North America and the world, this Members' Meeting is intended to become one focal point in the rededication of our Society to the goals of the 1923 Christmas Foundation Meeting. This means to resolve to ground our work in 'hearts which begin to have thoughts.' In recognition of our common tasks, the Dornach Vorstand joins us at this Meeting. Through our work together we may hope to take one further step in learning how to experience, practice, and sustain that sorely needed capacity, 'heart-thinking.'

A few sentences from the report by Ann Marshall, a member of the Society who was present on this occasion, may convey something of the mood of this event:

"While the emphasis upon man's life of feeling formed the body of each day, the Foundation Stone Meditation, in both English and German, became the true core or center, profoundly experienced and shared by all. There came not only a growing awareness of the full range and depth of Anthroposophy, but also, for many of us, a renewed commitment to the Foundation Stone continually rededicated in the heart of each individual member."

The early years of the 1980s proved to be decisive in the evolution of the anthroposophical movement in this country. As we know, they witnessed the transformation of the Society from a largely East Coast/West Coast to a genuinely "continental" membership community with Chicago as its pivotal point. And the May conference signaled the awakening of the realization that Anthroposophia would find her home in the "heart sphere" if she were to be not only "continental" but also truly human.

Outwardly, this transformation came to expression in the process of regionalization, and this was then followed in 1982 by the sale of the Society's headquarters in New York City, 211 Madison Avenue. The building had been purchased by the Society in 1945 but the New York members had come to take it for granted that it was, in fact, "theirs," and when, as will be described, circumstances made it necessary to sell the building, two local members were so outraged that they sued the Society to prevent the sale.

What triggered the decision to sell the building was the revocation by New York City of the building's tax exemption, which would have cost the Society $20,000 a year. This was a burden that the Society could not afford, nor were the New York members able to afford it. New York State law required that a membership society have official approval by its membership for the sale of a major asset, and this made it necessary for the Society to request approval from its members. As the Society's Secretary, Dietrich Asten wrote each of the Society's 1,890 members explaining the situation and requesting their permission for the sale. 1,263 members agreed to the sale, with nine dissenting, and, as a result, the Supreme Court of the State of New York approved the sale which was then

In the early 1980s

consummated at the price agreed upon of $1,350,000, which was divided equally between the Society and the New York Branch after all expenses had been taken care of.

Although the circumstances which led to the decision to sell 211 Madison Avenue were initially external to the Society, the consequences of the decision, and of the actual sale on August 2, 1982, had positive consequences both for the Society and for the Movement as a whole, as well as for the activity in New York City itself. In the broader context, the sale proved to be essential to the process through which the Movement was gradually becoming more truly continental and, in addition, it awoke the New York membership to the need for the establishment of active local initiative to form a responsible Branch.

The consequence was the Society's decision to move the national Library and—at least for the present—the Society's office as well. In the immediate vicinity of Harlemville, where Hawthorne Valley was becoming a thriving community and with Great Barrington directly across the Massachusetts border to the east, a building was available which could meet the immediate needs. Meanwhile, the Chicago Branch declared itself ready to provide a home for the Society's office, if, and when, it was ready to make the move. Although not in Chicago, the Society's office is now well located in Ann Arbor, Michigan, while the national Library continues to serve the membership and interested friends from its location in Harlemville, New York.

Publications

At various stages of my life I found myself preoccupied with and inspired by certain themes. Some of these eventually found their way to publication. On my return to America in 1940, after my seven years in Europe, I was fortunate to have the opportunity to publish an article in a periodical that existed for a brief period in those years. The article was entitled "Switzerland, Fortress of Freedom," published in *Tomorrow*,

Volume Two, Number 1, September 1942. As the title suggests, the article characterized Switzerland as the unique "island" of peace and freedom in the heart of war-torn Europe. It was in this article that I was able to refer to Albert Steffen (poet-dramatist and President of the General Anthroposophical Society with its headquarters at the Goetheanum in Dornach, Switzerland) and to the address he held at the Goetheanum on September 3, 1939, the day on which England and France declared war on Germany following Hitler's attack on Poland. Europe then found itself engulfed in the Second World War. Steffen began his address by saying:

> "Even if we ourselves should be swept away, let us create things of such permanence that they will survive without us. Let us not fool ourselves by thinking that the war began today, nor that it will end with any so-called peace treaty unless the world finds its way to ideas that are the source of genuine social reconstruction in accordance with the facts of economic, political and spiritual reality."

It was during the later years of the 20th century that I became aware of an observation by Rudolf Steiner that both puzzled and impressed me. On January 23, 1923, speaking to a gathering in Stuttgart, Germany, shortly after the destruction of the First Goetheanum in Switzerland, Steiner characterized the way in which Anthroposophy is able, and wishes, to enter life, by citing two examples. They were the form and structure of the First Goetheanum and the ways in which the Waldorf School was founded and conducted its affairs. What did these two examples have in common? What relevance might they have for us today? From one point of view they appeared to have nothing to do with one another, but the fact that Rudolf Steiner chose these two apparently so unrelated examples to illustrate how Anthroposophy wants to enter life today intrigued me greatly and I decided to pursue the question to try to understand what led Steiner to the observation. The more I wrestled with this apparent paradox, the more I came to realize that there was real significance hidden in it and that it deserved to be understood. The essay that emerged proved to be of genuine interest to some of my colleagues in the school movement and eventually led to its publication by the Pedagogical Section Council of the

School of Spiritual Science in North America. In consequence, it seems appropriate to include a reference to it here. The booklet was entitled: *The Third Space/The First Goetheanum and the First Waldorf School/What had they in common? Is there relevance here for us today?*

The First Goetheanum was a structure in which two domes of unequal size intersected to form an architectural whole. The larger dome, housing the auditorium, faced west and the smaller one, facing east, housed the stage. Both domes were sheathed in Norwegian slate which reflected the light and shadows of the surrounding sky. The larger dome was supported by seven pairs of wooden columns, each pair crowned by a carved capital which metamorphosed from a quiet, open form (Saturn) that conveyed a sense of potentiality, to increasingly complex forms climaxing in the fourth pair (Earth/Mars) and then unfolding in a more musical flow to the final pair which framed the stage. All seven pairs of capitals were united by a sculptured architrave which flowed forward above them. The smaller dome above the stage was carried by twelve columns of equal height, each with a throne-like carved wooden seat at its base. But the visitor, I believe, would only gradually have discerned the sculptured forms in the tides of color which greeted him as he entered the auditorium from the west and stood under the organ loft at the rear of the hall. The colors flooded the interior space from the curved ceiling painted in flowing colors which intensified from quieter shades immediately overhead, to stronger, brighter colors at the ceiling's height and then descended to richer, warmer colors approaching the stage. And into this movement of color, images were painted which spoke a language of their own. But it was not only the color which flooded the interior of the hall from above. Especially if it were a bright day, the sunlight poured through the mighty triptychal windows of engraved colored glass set in the outer wall to the visitor's right (to the south) as well as the quieter color shades on the left, to the north. The first window of a clear light green, the second of a crystalline blue, the third of a delicate lavender, and the fourth of a peach blossom-rose, poured their light from right and left, illuminating the passageway curving down between the outer wall and the columns supporting the dome, surrounding the many rows of wooden seats of the auditorium. Visitors who shared their memories of this extraordinary building, which stood, completed, for so very few years on the Dornach hill, also remembered the interplay of colors when the light from the outer windows struck, for instance, the back of one's hand, casting a shadow of a complementary color.

To return to the "Third Space," the speaker's podium was located directly below the intersection of the two domes that created a "threshold" between the "seven-space" of the auditorium beneath the larger dome, and the "twelve-space" of the stage below the small dome. One needs to recognize that there is a potential conflict hidden within this structure. Two potential tyrannies are hidden here. If the speaker—devoted student of spiritual science that he might very well be—is convinced that he has researched a truth, which he is determined to impose upon his audience, what might be characterized as a dogmatic "theocratic tyranny" is created. And, if the visitor who has entered the auditorium out of curiosity to know what goes on in this unusual building is determined to project his or her personal opinions, rather than being open to the thoughts and experiences that have arisen within the "twelve-space" below the small dome, then no "give and take," no genuine conversation can occur, and what might be characterized as a "democratic tyranny" holds sway. It is in this sense, I believe, that the recognition of the essential reality of the "third space" alone can create the freedom which must be present if the experience is to be truly human. Only if the speaker can allow the spiritual truth which he has researched "to die within him" and can then wait to see whether it "comes to life" in the minds and hearts of his audience does he leave his listeners free. And only if his hearers are able, and willing, to put aside their personal opinions and can open themselves to the possibility that a point of view that may challenge their preconceived convictions may, indeed, be valid does a genuine "conversation" take place. And it is in this sense that the recognition of the essential role of the "third space" can lead to genuine cultural freedom, thus creating the possibility for anthroposophical spiritual science to enter into the world and find its own life.

It was out of this recognition that Emil Molt, owner-director of the Waldorf-Astoria cigarette factory in Stuttgart, Germany, and a longtime student of Rudolf Steiner's work, turned to Rudolf Steiner on April 23,

1919, and asked whether he would found, and guide, a school which could offer the children of his employees an education which could enable them to grow up to be free human beings rather than limiting them as members of their proletarian class. And it was the same conviction that prompted Steiner to recognize that, in such a school, the children's teachers should have the freedom to organize and guide the school. For Steiner expected the teachers to work out of deeper insight into the forces at work in child development, and he knew that they would only succeed if they were able to creatively transform such insights in such a way that the students and parents could whole-heartedly accept them. Thus I came to see that, in this sense, the teachers in Waldorf schools, like the speaker in the Goetheanum, occupy a unique "third space" freely mediating between a world of profound spiritual insights on the one hand and, on the other, a world in which everyone is rightly entitled to their own opinion.

In the final years of the 20th century, Robert McDermott, with the financial support of Laurance Rockefeller, initiated the Vista Series dedicated to the work of Rudolf Steiner, published by the Anthroposophic Press. Robert asked me to contribute Steiner's biography as Volume One in the Series, a challenge which I gladly undertook. This resulted in *A Life for the Spirit/Rudolf Steiner in the Crosscurrents of Our Time*, published in 1997 by the Anthroposophic Press. Another early volume in the Vista Series was René Querido's *A Western Approach to Reincarnation and Karma/Selected Lectures and Writings by Rudolf Steiner*.

A Life for the Spirit turned out to be a volume of 263 pages with an appendix and annotated bibliography for further reading. It includes an introduction to the Vista Series by Robert McDermott as well as an introduction by the author in which I describe the path which led me to anthroposophy and to Rudolf Steiner's work. My introduction concludes with a section entitled "In Search of a New Thinking" which begins with the following paragraphs:

"Can we, from our vantage point at the end of the twentieth century and the beginning of the twenty-first, learn to read the reality underlying the complex chaos of events on life's surface? Can we discover a *seeing thinking* that truly distinguishes outer events from their deeper causes? Can we learn to read individual events as symptoms of the historical currents struggling for expression beneath the surface? These events cry out to be understood, because they are born from the social and spiritual needs of our time.

One of the greatest pioneers to have blazed a path to the source of such a thinking was Rudolf Steiner. This book is an attempt to trace how the path recognized and described by Steiner was also the one he himself followed in his individual biography. In doing this we will also touch on some of the practical results of his extraordinary insights."

This introductory section concludes with the following paragraph:

"We will meet Rudolf Steiner in the watershed year of the twentieth century, 1917. His entire work, however, stands within the tides of the century as a whole and leads us far into the next and beyond. He challenges us to think in ways that can engage the heart and will, as well as the mind."

Looking back on the experience of writing *A Life for the Spirit*, I realize that this experience awoke in me the seed of love for this human being which has ripened in me over the years.

On January 4, 1989, Arvia MacKaye, devoted wife of Karl Ege in their later years, passed away quietly in her home in Hillsdale, New York. It had been her ardent wish that she might hold the published edition of the life story of her parents Percy and Marion MacKaye, *The Power of the Impossible*, on which she had worked for many, many years. She had been urged and encouraged to write their life story by Percy MacKaye's Swiss poet-friend Albert Steffen. Unfortunately, this was a satisfaction that Arvia was not destined to enjoy. It was only three years later that, thanks to the energy and determination of her younger sister, Christy MacKaye Barnes, and to the generous support of a number of friends, and to the initiative taken by Bond and Thea Wheelwright to establish the Kennebec River

Press in Falmouth, Maine, that this remarkable volume finally appeared in print. Due, in part, to the circumstances of its publication and to the size and cost of the volume itself, *The Power of the Impossible/The Life Story of Percy and Marion MacKaye* never reached the audience that it deserved.

It was then, at the turn of the century, that I was asked by Bodo von Plato of the Forschungsstelle Kulturimpuls (Research Institute for Cultural Impulses) in Heidelberg, Germany, to contribute a brief biographical sketch of my father-in-law Percy MacKaye to be included in a monumental publication: *Anthroposophie im 20. Jahrhundert* (*Anthroposophy in the 20th Century*) *Ein Kulturimpuls in Biographischen Portraits* (*A Cultural Impulse in Biographical Portraits*), to be published by the Verlag am Goetheanum. As I became involved in the research necessary for this brief biographical sketch I began to realize how important it would be for readers in the new century to meet, and get to know, creative individuals, especially in the arts, in the previous century. This inspired me, drawing on Arvia's significant work, to write a much shorter, more easily accessible biography of Percy MacKaye.

This little book, *Percy MacKaye, Poet of Old Worlds and New,* was published in 2000 by Adonis Press, founded in 1941 by Arvia MacKaye for the publication of English translations of works by Albert Steffen and other anthroposophical authors and more recently, under the leadership of my son John, dedicated to the publication of Goethean, phenomenological science. In the preface I wrote:

> "Percy MacKaye was one of those who planted seeds of creative, artistic initiative in the cultural soil of the western world at the end of the nineteenth and in the early years of the twentieth century. The years that followed rolled relentlessly over the plowed ground, pressing the seeds deep into forgetfulness. It may be, however, that the time has now come for these seeds to sprout.
>
> The biographical sketch which follows here seeks to bring Percy MacKaye, and a few of those most closely associated with him, to the awareness of today's pioneers who are plowing new ground in the twenty-first century. Of special interest in this regard is Percy's

dedication to the ideal of community drama. His great pageant-masques involved thousands of amateur, volunteer participants, acting alongside their professional counterparts, and were witnessed by tens of thousands in St. Louis, New York City, Cambridge, MA, and Washington, DC. Writing about the impact of the Shakespeare Tercentenary masque, *Caliban of the Yellow Sands*, performed in the Lewisohn Stadium in New York City in 1916, a leading New York daily paper observed: 'Such an achievement is surely a foretaste of the eventual realization of the democratic ideal, where art will be made not only for the people, but also *by the people*, and all the people will cooperate to make the common life more beautiful, until the communal life itself shall become a living work of art'."

The culmination of my work as an author was *Into the Heart's Land/ A Century of Rudolf Steiner's Work in North America* published by Steiner Books in the summer of 2005: a monumental work of 622 pages, with 34 pages of notes and appendices. Well illustrated, and well-received, this was the fruit of four years of wonderfully rewarding work, for which I—as the old author—will always be sincerely grateful. It opened the door to so many new friends and colleagues, and, very specially, to an ever-ripening appreciation for the one, without whom it would never have been written. This is expressed in the opening paragraphs in the "Acknowledgments" with which the book begins:

"During the four years of work on this history, my respect, admiration, and gratitude has grown and deepened immeasurably for the individual without whose lifework this history would not exist. This is not only Rudolf Steiner as spiritual scientist but also as the human being one comes to know, directly and indirectly, through these pages."

Into the Heart's Land received many appreciative and discerning reviews of which the following paragraph by Douglas Sloan, Professor of History and Education, Teachers' College, Columbia University, NY and Sunbridge College, Spring Valley, NY (now retired) may serve as a much appreciated example:

"As indicated in its subtitle, this book by Henry Barnes is a history of the growth of Anthroposophy in North America since its introduction here at the beginning of the twentieth century. The work is a remarkable accomplishment; it could even be described as magisterial. In his introduction, Henry Barnes leads off with a question: 'How has Anthroposophy fared in the New World?' The book that follows is his effort to answer this question as fully as possible in one volume. In doing so, he has achieved what every historian seeks: a combination of a breadth of scope that is engaging and significant combined with a richness of detail that is always interesting, and that brings out again and again many diverse—often little known, at least they were to this reader—events, persons, and issues involved in the history of the movement. As suggested by its evocative title, *Into the Heart's Land*, both the outer cultural-institutional and the inner soul-life of the history of Anthroposophy in North America are presented in the story told here. ... The richness of the account is not only a gift to the general reader, but will also make this book an indispensable resource, a necessary starting point (a veritable *vade mecum*), for anyone in the future who undertakes to write a specialized history of any particular aspect of Anthroposophy in North America."

* * *

Realizing that important aspects of my life have been omitted and that they may be seen more objectively through the eyes of others, I gratefully include here the memories of some of my friends, former students and colleagues as well as those of my daughter Marion and son John.

I will then complete my autobiographical sketch with a chapter on my old age. This will then lead on to brief portrayals of the two individuals without whom my life-story would not be complete.

Memories of Friends, Family, Former Students and Colleagues

Anne Stockton

(Anne Stockton has been painting professionally for most of her life. She has taught for many years in the United States and in England, where she co-founded the Tobias School of Art. Currently, she lives and works in her studio in Sussex, England.)

Henry Barnes and I grew up together—he, a year younger, more a friend and schoolmate of my brother, Peter King Stockton. Henry was a jovial companion with a quiet sense of humor and went with my brother sailing, playing tennis, to the movies, Coney Island, and exchanging visits. I tagged along sometimes on their adventures, but was more often the older sister pioneering the mysteries of growing up.

Henry shared many things in our lives, particularly the American offshoot of the Moscow Art Theater, the American Laboratory Theater, which my family was engaged in bringing to the American theater scene. He even saved his pocket money to buy shares in the enterprise. It was part of his loyal nature which made him a friend for life.

I was invited one Thanksgiving when Henry served the meal and solemnly presented us each with seven kernels of sweet corn, saying "this in remembrance of the very first Thanksgiving," empathizing with those first American settlers.

He spent his last high school year in a boarding school in Arizona and from there entered Harvard University. Peter followed one year later. Some of their friends were already there, and Peter joined them as a freshman when they became sophomores. Henry and Peter roomed together during Peter's sophomore year. Peter was a manly but sensitive young man, writer and poet that he was, graduate of a day school, the avant-garde

Lincoln School of Teachers College, Columbia. But he was not one of the fashionable boarding school cliques at Harvard. Peter became the victim of their Bully-Gang, which included their old friends! He became a victim of the *mass* with hatred of what is *individual*. The result was the tragedy of which Henry has written. This changed our lives.

My mother had read some of Rudolf Steiner's writings while she carried my brother, and after his death she turned to them again, which helped to answer some of her burning questions. Henry and I shared this awakening to a new world of thought. We attended lectures together, and Henry gave my mother a substitute son's support through the following years. He discovered Rudolf Steiner's Waldorf method, and took himself to the Teacher Training program in Stuttgart, Germany. Teachers in Stuttgart have told me how amazed they were to find "out of America, a 'natural born' Waldorf teacher!"

He went from Stuttgart to England, sacrificing a high profile job in one of the elite schools in the States to teach in the English Steiner School 'Michael Hall,' pausing during those years for a romance or two. Henry went on to Dornach where he did meet a thicket of controversies to overcome, but, also, where he found his true life-companion, Christy MacKaye. Their long and distinguished life together was dedicated to Anthroposophy, Education and the Arts. Before Henry returned to America, Dr. Lehrs, one of the original Waldorf teachers, questioning him, was also amazed at his gifts and understanding of this 'education as an art,' and Henry said uncharacteristically, "It seems I just know instinctively what to do." Dr. Lehrs asked, "How old are you, Henry?" "Twenty-eight" "Then beware, that is the time your old karma runs out and you face creating of new!"

Henry became a teacher at the Steiner School in New York, and soon, Chairman of the Faculty. In his middle years he could hardly be called a teacher but a true Educator, pioneering Waldorf Education throughout the United States. At the time he entered it, the Steiner School was a small primary on the West Side of Manhattan. With his help, and the interest of Francis Edmunds, his mentor in England, he built up a full school with a successful high school on 79th Street.

We also had the questionable privilege of sitting together for some years on the Council of the Anthroposophical Society. How difficult it was to find people who could work together at all, let alone harmoniously. Here *individuality* is subject to many interpretations.

Later Henry offered me a job in the growing School. I was supposed to be the Registrar, which I enjoyed for all the different people I had to meet. For the next fourteen years I found myself with a desk in Henry's office as we interviewed new candidates. Through those years I marveled at his patience in working through school problems: with authorities, but mainly human problems with teachers and parents and children—and me, as I sat telephoning across the room from him! As a child I remember once trying to have a mud fight with Henry—anything to rouse some fury in him. I never saw him lose his temper. I was especially impressed once when I told him of a waiting appointment outside. He looked at his watch saying, "No, they are six minutes early. Ask them to wait" and he unflappably put his six minutes to good use.

We—Christy, Henry and I—kept in touch through the years, he in America and I then in England; and unfailingly, on January 18th I would have a letter from him sharing thoughts of and for my brother Peter, speaking of the ideals for which they both went through so much. There was something as of knights about both of them, or Parsifal seeking the grail. The best of America lived in them, which of late has been trod on as the Bully-Gang trod on my brother and his poems.

One thing struck me as the years of January 18ths rolled by, Henry living out his life and my brother not. I realized as I thought how true Henry's life had been to the ideals shared with my brother, that in the dedication to the deepest purposes of Anthroposophy, Henry had been living out my brother's life with his.

Marion MacKaye Ober

(The daughter of Henry Barnes, Marion Ober is an artist specializing in printmaking. She lives in Boston.)

My brother and I (and for much of the time my cousin Kathryn as well) had the not always openly appreciated privilege of growing up in the midst of this "constellation" of remarkably different personalities, each quite powerful in his or her own way. In the winter, my extended family lived at "410," the brownstone on East 84th Street in Yorkville, bought with the last of my grandmother's once extensive fortune. I have always had the feeling, although my father has never talked about his background much, that the loss of the family fortune in the financial crash in the twenties was rather a relief to him, and he always seemed to bear with equanimity our somewhat cramped quarters (my aunt and uncle and grandmother upstairs, the four of us and a constant group of my brother's and my friends downstairs), my mother's decidedly eccentric and rather absent minded cooking (when she could smell the baked potatoes burning, supper was ready), the marathon cleanings and re-fixings in order to rent out the furnished rooms on the two top floors, and the fairly lively atmosphere of a neighborhood still very much of immigrants and small shops where all neighbors felt it their duty to open windows and reprimand the noisy bunch of kids who ran freely in the back yards because the fences were down. My father lived amid all this with seeming equanimity; but he carries in his very being a sense of order and self-discipline, which gave measure to what might otherwise have been chaotic. There were moments, when faced with a house full of children playing hide and seek in every corner, or yet another deep, prolonged conversation over important ideas with Arvia, or yet another crisis on the phone from one school parent or another, when my father could make clear in a quiet and decided way, that he had had enough, it was time to bring this particular game or crisis to an end.

In the summers we were wonderfully lucky to have my mother's hillside childhood home in New Hampshire. Here too were an extended family of decided characters: my grandfather, flamboyant and dramatic;

my great Uncle Benton, wry, perceptive and curmudgeonly, and my Uncle Robin, lover of birds and long walks, but certainly inwardly off center from a worldly point of view. All were often there all summer. Nevertheless, it was an oasis where my father could spend time writing letters, gardening and building stone walls, where my mother had time to read and write, to make pickles and jams and sew clothes for herself and for me, and my brother, my cousin and I, after finishing chores, had hours in the woods and fields before each day ended with my grandfather or Uncle Benton and, in later years, my mother reading to us from the likes of Huck Finn, The Prisoner of Zenda or Lorna Doone.

It is wonderful now as my father nears his 96th birthday to have Cornish as a place where children, grandchildren and great grandchildren can gather during the summer to celebrate birthdays and weddings and have time with him there.

I think my overriding sense of my father is one of fairness, and behind this judicious and conscious respect for others, a deepening kindness. I think of the care with which he organized birthday celebrations for my mother, which allowed others to come forward and recognize her gifts, and the solidness of his understanding of her importance in his life. I think of the consciousness with which he listens for the thread of genuine seeking in the life histories of his former students and colleagues, his grandchildren, and yes, in mine. I think of the thoughtfulness with which he remembers some daily task, which lifts the burden of his own care or that of someone near him just a little—but steadily, and every day. My father's inner life and his lovingness are not based on immediacy and inspiration, but on daily attention and deepening consciousness.

John Michael Barnes

(John Barnes is a Waldorf teacher, writer and editor-in-chief of Adonis Press. He lives in Hillsdale, New York.)

I remember by father washing the large double-hung windows in our old brownstone house at 410 East 84th Street. The windows became very dirty, and my father took great pleasure in wiping them clean. We lived on the two lower floors, and we children had access to the back yard. My Aunt Arvia and her husband Karl Ege lived on the floor above us, which was conveniently connected to our apartment through an internal staircase. My father rented out the two top floors, which, I imagine, paid the mortgage. I can remember helping my father carry bedsteads and mattresses from the basement storage space up to the tenants' apartments.

My aunt was a night owl. Late at night, when my father finally came home from school, it was not unusual to hear my Aunt's quiet but insistent voice calling from the top of the stairs into our living room: "Henry? Do you have a minute?" A lengthy consultation about very important matters inevitably ensued—a tribute to my father's inner equanimity and endurance.

Sometimes I walked to school with my father in the morning. We were generally the first to arrive at the building at 15 East 79th Street, and my father would unlock the heavy outside door with its intricate ironwork and then the inside door that led to the large entrance hall with its white marble floor and elegant marble stairway. On at least one such occasion, finding the hall had not been cleaned the night before, my father mopped the marble floor himself. After school events he was usually the last to leave the school, making sure that chairs had been properly stacked, floors were swept, and everything was ready for the next morning. My father seemed to take full responsibility for the school.

In 8th Grade, our class took dancing lessons which culminated in a formal dance in the school's assembly room. I remember dancing with one of the girls in my class. The lights were dim, the mood romantic, and, holding me close in a moment of intimacy, she confided: "Your father makes me feel *so* safe!"

At our summer home in Cornish, New Hampshire, my father would usually spend his mornings dealing with "business." We would hear his typewriter clacking away. Then he would appear with a number of letters and carry them up the driveway to the mail box. In the afternoons he would put on his work boots, and I would help him clear the wilderness that was encroaching on our house. I remember him chopping down sizable pitch pines with an ax, pausing occasionally to catch his breath. Then I would help him lop off the branches and drag them to the large burn pile. My sister and I loved to play in and bounce on the piles of springy, aromatic pine boughs. Then there were the tough honeysuckle bushes that had to be pulled or conquered with clippers, root by root. Other favorite pastimes of my father's were working in the flower or vegetable gardens. We had a wonderful compost pile. I remember how my father would sift last year's compost through a finely-meshed woven iron bedspring. We plunged our hands into the resulting pile of soft, rich, dark earth and carried it off to the garden in the wheel-barrow like a great treasure.

As I look back on my boyhood memories of my father, he was always working. I have no memory of his ever playing games of any kind. My father simply loved to work! But there were exceptions, particularly in the summer, when, having religiously swept the house on Saturday, we would have our festive Sunday gatherings with beautiful, fresh bouquets of flowers, candles, singing, a reading from the bible, a psalm, and the lord's prayer. Or our trips to the White Mountains to climb Mt. Washington. My father loved the majestic grandeur of the mountains.

I spent the last three and one half of my high school years in Germany, away from my family—and the school where my mother, father, aunt, godfather and godmother taught!
When I returned to go to college, I experienced my father in new ways while at home during vacation visits. I came to appreciate his way of withholding judgment. This was, I believe, an inborn tendency which he had further strengthened through conscious effort. At around 20 years of age, I had very strong opinions, but I also sensed that there were advantages to not jumping to premature conclusions. I could see how withholding judgment created a space in which wise decisions could ripen based on more complete insight.

Though I was sometimes frustrated by my father's reluctance to take a stand on some burning issue, I sensed that his reticence arose out of an inner strength and that it allowed for the possibility of yet unknown perspectives. This highly developed capacity of my father's made him a good listener and mediator. It inspired the trust of people who held diverse and disparate views, and this made him a good leader. I remember him saying: "Good administration can only be based on trust." He was someone who listened openly but was not easily swayed, someone whom one could trust to carry through on his commitments. More than most, he knew that trust had to be earned and cultivated and that this required a consciousness of and care for the whole organization, especially of all the people involved. He was keenly aware of the importance of good communication.

My father was never one to take an ideological stand on a given issue. Even though he was deeply convinced that education needed to be autonomous and free of state regulation, he nevertheless gladly supported the initiative of the Milwaukee public schools to create a public Waldorf school for inner-city children, and he enthusiastically helped in the training of the teachers who were preparing to teach at Milwaukee's Urban Waldorf School. He did so because he admired and trusted the key people involved in the initiative.

In the early 1950s the Rudolf Steiner School was facing an enrollment and financial crisis, and the Board found itself unable to take responsibility for the School's future. All of the faculty, however, wished to commit themselves to the future of the School. Thereupon the Board handed over the responsibility for the school to the faculty, and the main responsibility for the School was carried by the Faculty Council. The result was that, from that time forward, the school began to prosper. My father often noted this fact, yet he did not raise it to a general principle that all Waldorf schools should be run this way. He sought to base his judgments on concrete situations and truly practical solutions. He was very wary of abstract thinking and its tendency to make absolute demands.

My father also had a remarkable gift for public speaking. He never seemed to require notes. He had a very good memory, and his historical knowledge and the English language seemed to be entirely at his disposal.

When he spoke, his sentences and paragraphs were well organized and delivered with calm, well punctuated emphasis. A former student, Thomas Klein, noted recently:

"Three years ago (in 2005) I heard a lecture by Henry Barnes. When I closed my eyes it was as though I was again sitting in one of his main lessons at school. He had a wonderful, distinctive way of speaking as a teacher. Now, decades later, I was struck to hear him speak in exactly the same way."

My father was not a fiery speaker, nor did he entertain his audience with a display of rhetoric. Yet, even at age 95, at the funeral of his younger brother Alfred, he stood up and spoke with an eloquence that deeply moved all present. Even though my father was not one to crack jokes, he could, given the right occasion, tell some very funny ones that would set his listeners into peals of laughter.

I was often struck by the admiration with which people spoke of my father. I came to realize that this was not only because of his accomplishments but also because of the impression he made on others. His patrician upbringing and bearing no doubt helped to inspire the confidence of upper-class New Yorkers. But he also gained the genuine warm respect of the Chinese who laundered his shirts, of the clerk at the post office or the janitor at the School, an easygoing, gentle Black man. He was one of those people whose presence immediately filled the space when he entered a room. Though he was neither arrogant nor pompous, he did possess a commanding presence and could, on occasion, be very forceful when his mind was made up. It is perhaps no coincidence that he was born on August 12th, under the sign of Leo.

In this connection I am reminded of an incident that occurred in Central Park, not far from the Rudolf Steiner School and 79th Street. A teenage youth turned on my father with a knife, demanding his wallet. My father looked the youth straight in the eyes and sternly told him to put his knife away, whereupon the would-be thief turned tail and ran away.

Even though—or perhaps because—he was the one upon whom so many relied, there were times when my father was brought to the breaking point. I remember this happening when he was in his late

60s and came close to snapping under the weight of his various and heavy responsibilities for the new initiative in Harlemville and for the Anthroposophical Society. Hidden to most of those who took his seemingly inexhaustible positivity and strength for granted was the extraordinary, almost desperate effort that he sometimes had to make to rise to the challenges that came to meet him.

Though my father was blessed with a strong constitution, robust health and keen intellectual capacities, he would not have been able to accomplish what he did in life had it not been for his inner work on the path of self-development outlined by Rudolf Steiner. Alongside his many outer commitments, he faithfully devoted a certain amount of time on a daily basis to this work. For many years he was a reader of the First Class of the School for Spiritual Science. He continues to live intensely with the verses of Rudolf Steiner's *Calendar of the Soul* throughout the yearly rhythm of the seasons. Though he rarely speaks about his meditative work, it is clear from comments he has made that an important aspect of his inner striving has been and remains the cultivation of the "middle realm" of the heart, the center of our humanity. When asked about his inner work, his brief response was always steeped in the greatest humility. Nevertheless, it was without doubt this regular inner striving and the example of Rudolf Steiner's own life and work that gave him the spiritual strength to succeed in his endeavors.

Dorit Winter

(Dorit Winter, Rudolf Steiner School class of 1964, is an author and director of the Bay Area Center for Waldorf Teacher Training in San Rafael, California.)

It is 1961, the centenary of Rudolf Steiner's birth, and I, a 14 year-old, have been dragged to a big exhibition in a hotel downtown. I am a 9th grader at a public junior high school in Queens, and my mother, an anthroposophist, is thinking about finally transferring my brother, Amos, to the Rudolf Steiner School in Manhattan. Amos has been having trouble at his elementary school; our childhood in South Africa had not prepared him to play baseball, and this sin could not be forgiven by his 5th grade classmates nor by his teacher.

The big room at the hotel is filled with tables, and in spite of my skepticism I am drawn toward all the beautiful things. There is a noticeable mood about all these hand made objects. My mother goes over to talk to the man behind the table with the brochures, while I wander down the aisles of wooden candle holders, knitted socks, paintings, and odd format books with large pages covered in colorful handwriting, diagrams, illustrations, calligraphy, and compositions which I start to read.

The man behind the table has evidently been watching me, because he calls me over and asks me what I think. I take a good look at him, trying to decide what he wants, but all I see is a good natured face waiting for an answer. I admit I am impressed.

On the way home, my mother tells me that the man behind the desk thinks that if Amos comes to the school, I should go, also. And so I do.

Some weeks later I am surprised to find out that the man behind the desk is the head of the school (they don't say principal, they say "chairman"). But the initial encounter remains vivid in my mind to this day. He must have seen past the haughty 14 year-old, and noticed that she was taken by the display of beautifully made things. And so he becomes a prime agent in my destiny.

It is my first semester at the Rudolf Steiner School. I have already had a physics block with a teacher the likes of whom I have never before experienced. During his main lesson block, I become aware that he is always talking about more than what he is talking about. Of course I cannot exactly articulate this, but there is such an earnestness in his presentations that somehow the topics become compelling. Now it is Mr. Barnes in front of the room, and he is describing Mesopotamia. He is talking about cuneiform and ancient repositories of clay tablets, about Gilgamesh, and about the Fertile Crescent. I am mesmerized by his hands. They are also talking. And his voice. His sentences are like something carved in stone. Again I understand, without understanding what I understand, that Mr. Barnes is telling us more than he is telling us. Later, as a 12th grader, I sculpt a hand out of clay. I am secretive about the model. It is Mr. Barnes. Two decades later, when I am teaching history of art to the 9th graders at the brand new Great Barrington Rudolf Steiner High School, I remember again those classes with Mr. Barnes that impressed themselves on me as indelibly as a chisel in dry clay. He was telling us, without telling us, about the third post-Atlantean era.

I am out of graduate school. Some 9 years have passed since my high school graduation ('64) and I am back in Manhattan. I am to teach German at the Rudolf Steiner School—grades 5 though 11. High school students have a choice of Russian, French and German. The German classes take place in the library. One day during that first year I enter the library to find Mr. Barnes sitting in a corner, a big book in his lap. He is leafing through it. My students come in. We get through the class. Next day Mr. Barnes is there again. Strange, I think, that he needs to be reading in here now. During my class he never once looks up. I carry on. On the 3rd day, as he leaves, he grins at me. Only then do I realize that he has been there to "observe" the new German teacher.

During the 7 years that I teach at the school, Mr. Barnes evolves into Henry. At first I find it almost impossible to address him that way. My respect and affection for Mr. Barnes is colossal. How can I call him anything else? But one summer during a conference in Harlemville, I find myself next to him hoeing some newly turned earth, and after that it seems easier. It is during that summer, too, that one day at lunch, I and two friends "perform" a skit for Mr. and Mrs. Barnes—that is, Henry and Christy. My two friends and I had been to an AWSNA conference where we had prepared, but never performed, a "Waldorf Travel Agency" skit. It was full of corny jokes and bad puns, with lines like, "Waldorf salad choc full of nuts." Henry and Christy laugh 'til they cry.' It is marvelous.

As I took on more responsibilities at the school, and became aware of the inner workings of things, I often found myself looking to Henry. He and I would walk home in the same direction from 15 East, and although we rarely talked about any issue or event directly, his keen interest in my struggles supported and encouraged me. I was a new teacher. Fifth graders could reduce me to tears. High school students were only a few years younger than I was. I was in my 20's and had little patience for endless meetings, yet found myself chairing more and more of them. Henry watched me at a distance, like a benevolent uncle, saying the right word at the right time. He was like a guardian, helping me even when I didn't know I needed help, steering me along at a time when I felt sovereign, yet had so much to learn. Especially in the realms of Waldorf pedagogy and anthroposophy, realms I had not previously met formally, he was a clear and illuminating inspiration.

Later, when I moved to Great Barrington, Henry and Christy were neighbors in Harlemville. Henry was the local reader for First Class, and I consider myself very fortunate to have had that same sonorous voice, which so impressed me as a teenager, introduce me to the Lessons. Nor can I count it as a coincidence.

When my life in Great Barrington came unraveled, Henry visited me and put things in perspective. He took my life's path seriously, and gave me hope.

As part of that unraveling, I became a patient at the Ita Wegman Klinik in Arlesheim. During my first week at the clinic, I heard a knock at the door and lo, there stood Henry in the doorway behind a great bouquet of flowers. He assured me that there would be a way of finding money for this hiatus. Unbeknownst to me, he spoke to people in Dornach and at the clinic, and made arrangements....

In recent years, after he moved to the Fellowship in Spring Valley, he and my mother were neighbors. She bore him great affection, and often commented on the fact that he seemed like a relative. During the many visits I had with him in his impressively tidy room, he never failed to ask about my latest doings with the same thoroughgoing interest he had always had. He was immensely encouraging. By his sheer example, he never failed to buoy my spirits.

Again and again, from that initial encounter in 1961, Henry has been an inspiration to me both personally and professionally. He has accompanied and assisted me as teacher, mentor, friend and "uncle" through many phases of my biography. I cherish that.

Carol Katz Williams

(Carol Katz Williams, Rudolf Steiner School class of '65, is a writer who lives in Sag Harbor on New York's Long Island.)

I first met Henry Barnes when he interviewed me for a place in the ninth grade at the Rudolf Steiner School in New York. I remember a tall, rather presidential-looking man behind a large desk. He asked me about the school in London that I had gone to till then, listened carefully to my answers, then explained some of the differences I would find if I came to the Steiner School. I had been interviewed at several other schools that week. Some representatives had spoken about their schools' high standards. At other schools I had been asked to make drawings, presumably to reveal my inner self. Mr. Barnes did neither. Our interview was simply a meeting, and I felt that I had been met.

There was much that confused and was difficult for me in making the transition from a very academic English school to one in which I carved wood and began eurythmy. There was nothing for which I am not now grateful. But I can say that during Mr. Barnes' history main lesson blocks, there was not one day when I did not wake in the morning thrilled to be going to school. My own children might find this hard to believe, but it was true. I will try to explain why this was and the golden thread this particular teacher wove through my four years of high school.

To begin with, as I realize now, Mr. Barnes had brilliant technique. He could evoke a time or a place or an individual with drama, humor, and profound seriousness. We sat at the edge of our seats, transported. Then just at the point where we might have become lost in his words—he would stop and turn the class around to us: "So, what do you think would happen next?" "Why do you think that?" "How do you know?" "How might you find out?" Our responses would fly across the room, hands waving, minds on fire. Beyond this was the almost uncanny way he seemed to address, in what he taught, who we were and what we were becoming.

Our ninth grade subject was Modern History, the great movements of national and human liberation from the nineteenth century to the present day. We began each class with a speech chorus from Edwin Markham's 'The Man with the Hoe,' asking in our collective roar:

O masters, lords and rulers in all lands,
Is this the handiwork you give to God,
This monstrous thing distorted and soul-quenched?
How will you ever straighten up this shape;
Touch it again with immortality?

To answer that question we studied the revolutions of 1848, the life of Garibaldi, the treaty of Versailles. As part of our homework we read the New York Times every day to understand the time in which we lived and the ways in which that question still waited to be answered, perhaps by us.

In tenth grade the perspective shifted to the distant past. Our study of the ancient civilizations of India, Persia, Mesopotamia, Palestine, and Greece began with descriptions of the particular geographies and climates. What kinds of cultures emerged in each place? Why? What were the religious and spiritual insights that emerged from Hinduism, Buddhism, Zoroastrianism, Judaism and Islam, Greek myths and mysteries? In what ways did they change humanity? Mr. Barnes set the scene with facts and dates, migration, invasions, myths and cosmology. We students questioned and investigated and wrote our first long research papers.

As the class took shape, each of these movements of peoples and consciousness no longer seemed separate or discrete, or even long ago. Instead each contributed its particular facet to a continually emerging process of awakening. Beyond feeding my intellectual curiosity about the past, I felt I was learning—confirming perhaps—something essential about life itself. This year I reread the chapter in Rudolf Steiner's "Occult Science" about the evolution of mankind in which, powerfully and bewilderingly, one grasps the sense of human capacities emerging towards freedom. Tenth grade history suddenly came strongly to my mind. Nothing was occult about those classes. They were all entirely accessible. And yet Mr. Barnes skillfully— and I suspect infinitely carefully—conveyed to my fifteen-year-old self the confidence that the world I live in is full of meaning, and movement and direction, and that the key to it lives within myself.

By the time our class reached eleventh grade we turned our newly developed investigative skills upon our own teachers. I do not know if this happens every year, but in 1964 it was practically inevitable. We challenged our teachers to tell us something about Rudolf Steiner and his anthroposophy. "The school is named after its inventor. Why don't you ever tell us about it?" As I recall, we were told, quite firmly, first that anthroposophy is difficult and we were too young to understand it, and second that it would be entirely inappropriate—an invasion of our freedom—if we were to be 'taught' anthroposophy. Naturally we were not satisfied at all.

Apparently we did not go completely unheard. In the twelfth grade, Mr. Barnes introduced the Senior Seminar. We sat, almost as equals, around the table in the library, endeavoring to match our teacher's seriousness and grasp the time in which we lived, how it had come to be, and what parts we might come to play in it. The part of the seminar I remember best was when we were given short passages from Karl Marx and Friedrich Engels' "The Communist Manifesto," Adolf Hitler's "Mein Kampf" and Rudolf Steiner's "Three-Fold Social Order" to read. We were asked to try to suspend anything we knew about the respective authors and their roles in history and to focus instead only on a careful analysis of the rhetoric. How is the argument framed? To what part of you is it addressed? How would you assess its truth? Mr. Barnes said little, but he listened carefully to each of us. He was asking us simply to notice. And I think what we noticed most of all was that we *could* notice. With that tool sharpened, we could read—or think—anything and remain inwardly free.

I see that in my account of the profound level at which Henry Barnes taught, he himself has almost disappeared behind his lessons. Rather than try to fill this gap, I remember reading that Steiner warned that if a high school teacher has unexamined personal traits, his adolescent students will be unable to hear him. I think that all of us heard Mr. Barnes very clearly. Moreover, we respected and loved him and felt sure he felt the same towards us.

Nick Lyons

(Nick Lyons is an author and longtime parent and supporter of the Rudolf Steiner School.)

I once heard Henry Barnes present a sample history class to parents. On that occasion my wife and I still knew little about Waldorf education. We had questions, and we wanted to see how this intriguing pedagogy worked. We heard a tall, mobile man with deep eyes that often laughed talk about the Russian revolutionary Lenin, his dramatic rise, his appearance before crowds, and even his appearance after death. It wasn't just talk; it was a *presentation*: impeccably clear and vivid, sharply dramatic, a seed to live in the imagination. The man before us, Henry Barnes, became his subject!

Virginia Sease

(Virginia Sease taught at Highland Hall Waldorf School in Los Angeles for many years. She has been a member of the Executive Council (Vorstand) of the General Anthroposophical Society at the Goetheanum in Dornach, Switzerland since 1984.)

I met Henry Barnes—in 1958 I believe it was—in Stuttgart, Germany, where he was visiting. I was taking the teachers' training course at the Stuttgart Waldorf School, and we met because he had heard that a young American was studying Waldorf education in Stuttgart.

There was a discussion at that time about my possibly coming to teach at the Rudolf Steiner School in New York City. This appealed to me very much, because I often was in New York City for my singing lessons. However, when Henry heard that just shortly before our conversation I had sent an acceptance to the Highland Hall Waldorf School, at that time situated in North Hollywood, California, he fell silent, but then said: "No, you have committed yourself to that Waldorf School, a pioneer Waldorf school, and that is what you should do."

My going to California meant that for a long time I did not see Henry Barnes again. Only many years later, in the mid-seventies, when I was sent to New York City for a meeting of the Association of Waldorf Schools in North America, did Henry and I meet again.

The meeting was held at the Rudolf Steiner School in Manhattan, and there I became aware of how integrated Henry Barnes was in that particular school. He was the guardian of the school, he was the impulse-giver of that school, and he held the love and the respect of all of the teachers whom I met then and on my subsequent visits to New York City.

In the year 1979, at a pedagogical conference in Spring Valley, a few of the teachers who were also members of the First Class of the School of Spiritual Science met one evening to discuss whether it would be possible to begin ongoing work within the Pedagogical Section for those teachers who had decided to become members of the First Class.

Henry of course was part of that meeting which also included Werner Glass, Ekkehart Piening and myself.

At Michaelmas 1979, just a couple of months later, we met again in Dornach at the Goetheanum for the Michaelmas Conference. We spoke with Jörgen Smit, who was then the leader of the Pedagogical Section, and asked him whether it would be possible to start the Pedagogical Section in North America, and to form a council. Jörgen Smit was enthusiastic about this idea and gave us the green light. Later, after things were working in a very wonderful way with the Pedagogical Council and the inner work of the Pedagogical Section, we discovered that America was the first country— and at that time of course the only country—to have a Pedagogical Section and a Pedagogical Council.

All of us appreciated Henry's wise manner of looking at such things, and we agreed with him that no teacher should feel in any way excluded from anything of this nature. Therefore in the next years, he and I as Class Holders identified the teachers who were interested in finding out about the Pedagogical Section, and we took turns: one of us did something for the members of the First Class, and the other did something for the teachers who were not yet part of the First Class. But it was Henry's strong feeling that each teacher should feel totally welcome within the structures of the Waldorf School movement irrespective of his or her participation in the School of Spiritual Science.

One last anecdote before I turn to Henry's work within the Anthroposophical Society. One very cold winter night in New York City, when I was there for a meeting of the Association of Waldorf Schools in North America, Henry and Christy invited me to their home for dinner. We were speaking about the pressures on a Waldorf school teacher, about the many things one had to keep in mind beside all the preparation for the children. I asked Henry what his secret was, how he kept everything so well organized and always remained in command of the situation and so jovially complacent. His answer was: "I never go to bed at night without emptying out my briefcase and taking care of the things that have accumulated there during the day." A very good lesson for every teacher.

Let me now turn to Henry's role in the Anthroposophical Society. After I returned to the United States in 1959 I read in the "Weekly News" and the "News for Members" from the Goetheanum, which at that time was published every week in English translation by Dora Baker, that controversies were occurring within the Society in Europe. The controversies were of a serious nature. When I then asked people in the United States about this, they said: "Well, we don't understand it, but it's really terrible." When we came to speak about those difficulties, Henry, who was very involved from at least a spectator's point of view in the controversies within the Anthroposophical Society, even within the Executive Council of the Society, said that he had made up his mind that these difficulties and controversies should not cross the Atlantic Ocean. That meant that most Americans growing up in anthroposophy in those decades of the forties, fifties, sixties, even into the seventies of the last century, did not carry the burden of the conflicts that were going on in Europe; rather in America anthroposophy had the possibility of developing more freely between people of many different persuasions. This was true even for those who came from Europe and belonged to one or the other of the conflicting segments of the society.

Those problems were left behind. I think that one of the most important factors in the life of the Anthroposophical Society in America was that Henry was in a position not to allow these very divisive situations to influence the work in the English speaking New World.

As many people who experienced Henry know, he is a man of cultivated speech. He is, however, also a man of spontaneous, correct deeds. One example will suffice to show this side of his nature.

In the summer of 1978 the Class Holder for Los Angeles died rather suddenly, and the task came to the writer of this article. Henry immediately came out to Los Angeles in order to make sure that the transition of the responsibility from one Class Holder to the next would go in the right way. He stayed just a few days, but in those few days he also was able to build the bridge which was necessary so that the new Class Holder could take on this task. Also the instruction which was necessary for the task was communicated through Henry Barnes: A man of real action, not only of excellent speech!

In 1981 the Society in the United States had progressed to the point that three regions had been developed. From about 1977 on they had worked individually, and in 1981 the decision was made that each region would choose three representatives to form a council. Each of the three regions had its own method for that procedure. When it came to the Eastern region, the members discussed and suggested who should be the representative in the Eastern region, whereas in the West the regional council made the decision. As destiny would have it, the decision of the Eastern region happened to occur at Kimberton Farms while I was there, so I witnessed the process. A group of members and council members from the Eastern regional council had come together, and, after considering the suggestions of the membership, they agreed upon three people. Henry was present at that meeting, but he left the room while the decision was taking place so that his presence would not be an influence.

The three who were chosen were Carlo Pietzner, Dietrich von Asten, and Henry Barnes. There were discrepancies in regard to these three personalities as far as their manner of work was concerned, not however their personal relationship to each other. When Henry came back to the meeting, he was asked whether it was feasible for these three to take on the task. He responded: "We will be able to work together," and sure enough, that was indeed the case for three years until the sudden death of Dietrich von Asten.

That whole chapter in Henry's life within the Anthroposophical Society centers around his task as General Secretary of the Anthroposophical Society in the United States of America. He came regularly at least twice a year to the Goetheanum for the meetings of the General Secretaries. He was well ensconced in this position when I myself was called to the Vorstand in 1983 and then began my service in 1984.

During the meetings of the General Secretaries Henry always sat next to Brian Butler, the General Secretary from New Zealand. Brian Butler knew no German whatsoever. Henry's German, on the other hand, was quite perfect, and during the entire three days' meeting Henry would write down what everybody was saying on large pads of yellow paper and pass his notes to his neighbor, Brian Butler, so that he would be informed of what was occurring. This was a deed which all General Secretaries looked at with amazement and with gratitude as an example of real service to another human being.

In Europe, Henry Barnes was considered—not just because he was the General Secretary but because he is who he is—as an archetypal American, who possessed the additional advantage that he spoke and wrote German with perfection. He was regarded, one could say, as an individual within the leadership of the Anthroposophical Society who represented for the European participants all of the positive things which belong to the American heritage: Openness, kindness, tactfulness, friendliness, directness, without discrimination against any person regardless of their background.

To this day many people in Europe ask me about Henry Barnes, and they are always very happy if I can give them even a little morsel of information about him.

In conclusion I would like to mention that I am quite sure that all who know and have experienced Henry Barnes, who have been fortunate enough to have had Henry Barnes enter their lives, feel a continuing stream of warmth and support from him, a stream which, in some cases, was a lifeline when dealing with difficult tasks. He is truly a very special person. From my viewpoint, the fact that his destiny led him to Anthroposophy and to Waldorf education confirms the significance of the Anthroposophical Society and the Waldorf School movement, because in him we see a great individuality very connected with Rudolf Steiner who devotes himself to these high ideals and is also in a position to carry them out.

Old Age

As old age approached, Christy and I followed the advice of John and his wife Astrid and moved from our Hillsdale cottage "in the country" to the "metropolis" of Harlemville and gladly took up residence in the bungalow that John had converted from a small barn into an attractive little house directly behind their home in the "Red House." With this move we became "Harlemville residents" and were directly part of the community with which we had been connected since its inception in 1972. This was a happy situation for the aging couple, as we both retained a certain independence yet received the direct help and care we were in need of. It also meant that we could share in a more direct way in the life of the community. One of the consequences of our new situation was that we could have the help of community members, and, in particular, of students in the Hawthorne Valley high school, of which we were next-door neighbors.

As time passed, Christy and I realized that we would need more and more help and we also realized that this would be a burden on our family which we did not want to impose on them. Astrid had passed away in December 1996, and her daughter, Aurea Davis, generously offered to undertake our care. But, as we faced the reality of what this would mean for a young couple preparing to start their own family we wondered what the alternatives might be and our attention was drawn to the Fellowship Community in Spring Valley, New York, a two-hour drive south of Harlemville. And the more we learned about this community, the more we realized that it offered a truly human solution for the life and care of the aged that was directly inspired by the life and work of Rudolf Steiner, to which both Christy and I were wholeheartedly committed. And this led, in October 2001, to Christy's joining the Fellowship Community, where I joined her the following spring.

The Fellowship Community

Now situated on seventy-seven acres in suburban Rockland County within thirty miles of New York City, the Fellowship Community in 1996 was able to purchase the adjacent Duryea Farm, one of the very last farms in Rockland County. In consequence, the Community, in addition to its sixty-nine resident members, thirty-six full-time coworkers, and their children, and numerous volunteers and part-time helpers, now includes an old apple orchard, a thriving biodynamically composted and cultivated vegetable garden, a small milking herd and innumerable chickens and proudly crowing roosters.

What unites this community? What keeps us going? These are not, at first, easy questions to answer, but they are well worth exploring.

Three hearty, healthy meals a day, shared in a common dining room. A varied menu, not "institutionally cooked" but more truly home-like, serving fresh-grown biodynamic vegetables, with community-baked breads, cookies and cakes. Homemade yoghurt, delicious Fellowship granola, with raisins, prunes and wheat germ in home-cooked oatmeal every morning for breakfast. Salad at lunch and supper, with a different homemade salad dressing almost every day. Honey available each day for breakfast and at morning and afternoon snacks as well.

But this is not our only nourishment. There is music every day. And community chorus every Thursday morning led by a wonderfully experienced and enthusiastic former Waldorf choral director and music teacher, now a resident member of the Community.

Watercolor painting sessions open to all who want to participate every Wednesday and Friday morning; a sculpture studio available almost daily and, at noon, each Friday, the Hand and Hoe gift shop and gathering place is open for lunch and local sociability just down the hill at the entrance to the Community.

Directly across Hungry Hollow Road, the Threefold Auditorium offers eurythmy programs, occasional plays, concerts, lectures and entertainment. And a short walk leads to Sunbridge College and the Green

Meadow Waldorf School, the internationally recognized Eurythmy School, and the Natural Food Co-op, open seven days a week, where organic products of many kinds are available.

The Fellowship Community is housed in a number of buildings of which the central facility is Hilltop House, built in the mid-sixties of the twentieth century as the extension to what had, originally, been the home of Henry and Lisa Monges, overlooking Hungry Hollow Road.

The Community is genuinely cosmopolitan. Japan, Taiwan, and a number of European countries are represented. And, during the years that Christy and I have been resident members here, it has also included Russia as well as China. In fact, there is now a successful, groundbreaking Waldorf and anthroposophical initiative in Chengdu, China, where two former Fellowship coworkers are the pioneers.

But what is truly at the heart of the Fellowship? It is, I believe— whether we are all aware of it, or not—that the reality, described by Rudolf Steiner, of the human being as a threefold being of body, soul and spirit lives in the hearts of those who create the daily care, who enable the Fellowship to exist. And central to this understanding is the conviction that the organ that enables us to be truly human is the human heart.

For we, in the Western World, are easily will- and intellect-driven and what we need, above all, is to awaken, and nourish the forces of the human heart. And, in this connection, the Fellowship is a remarkable example in practical social life. This penetrates right down into the handling of economic affairs. As an example, the two physicians who provide medical care for the members of the Community, and, in addition, maintain a thriving general medical practice, do not, automatically, receive the personal income which they earn. As with all the Community coworkers, they receive what they need to maintain their lives, and the rest flows into the economic life of the Community. This is also one of the ways in which the Fellowship is able to offer its services at considerably less than is generally charged by eldercare facilities. The fact that the Fellowship Community exists today is thanks to the initiative of Dr. Paul Scharff, with the devoted support of his wife, Ann Scharff, who not only pioneered the initiative in the 1960s, but continue to guide and support it today. Chapter

44 in *Into the Heart's Land* describes the Fellowship Community and its history in greater detail, but, as a current member, I can only add this brief word of appreciation and gratitude to Dr. and Mrs. Scharff, as well as to all those who contribute, and have contributed to maintain and foster this remarkably human, and truly social initiative.

An initiative that has helped me to find myself as an inwardly nourished, inwardly growing individual in my life's closing years is my weekly participation in a circle which has engaged itself with a challenging theme: the understanding of the role of karma and reincarnation in human destiny as portrayed in the esoteric teaching of Rudolf Steiner. About thirty members and friends gather in the lovely Goethe Room, as the central meeting place is known, each Friday evening, under the guidance of Dr. Karnow—one of the Fellowship's two physicians—to study Steiner's lectures on karma and reincarnation. The study is conducted in a very open way. Everyone interested is welcome to participate. Questions are raised, insights and opinions are shared, without the slightest sectarian emphasis. As a student of Steiner's work for over seventy years, it is a real joy to be able to continue to deepen my understanding of life's challenging riddles in company with sincerely searching and interested friends.

In addition, a very special gift of the Fellowship Community in which we are privileged to participate are the memorial gatherings in which we are invited to share in the life-story of those members and friends who have crossed the threshold and have entered the life after death, so revealingly described by Rudolf Steiner in his anthroposophical studies. It can happen, on such an occasion, that one comes to know, and to meet, a dear friend with whom one may have shared life on a day-to-day basis, as if one were meeting him or her for the very first time in his innermost being.

Another remarkable initiative which has recently surfaced has come to be known as the "Otto Specht School" in which a number of members, several of whom had years of teaching experience, work with a group of youngsters in their pre-adolescent, and also somewhat later years who are struggling to cope with various developmental and learning difficulties. It is interesting to note that the use of the name Otto Specht refers to an experience that Rudolf Steiner describes in his autobiography when, as a young man in Vienna, he was engaged to tutor the sons of a local merchant; one of the sons was hydrocephalic and had developmental problems which, it was assumed, would limit his education to a minimum. His young tutor, however, recognized a latent intelligence in Otto, who was handicapped by a lack of physical and emotional strength which allowed him only the most limited ability to concentrate and learn. Steiner saw that he needed to engage him, initially, for very short periods and therefore developed a method in which he prepared the briefest of lessons that would slowly be extended and intensified. The result was that Otto Specht gradually lengthened and deepened his span of attention and eventually was able to attend university and qualify as a medical doctor. The Otto Specht School is another example of the social initiatives which have arisen and been supported and have become part of the ongoing creative human life of the Fellowship Community.

* * *

One of the many reasons for my sincere gratitude to find myself here at the Fellowship Community in my closing years is the fact that I can set out each morning after breakfast for a walk that leads me up the hill behind Hilltop House, past the chicken yard, and into the woods where a bench awaits me, where I can rest and enjoy the quiet solitude with the morning sun illuminating my surroundings from the east behind me. And I marvel at the mystery that I do not see the light until it strikes the trunks and branches of the trees around me, even though it is thanks to the sun's light that I see everything around me. How remarkable! I do not "see" the light until it strikes an object. Light is, in itself, invisible, although it illumines the whole world! And, as this thought awakens in me, another thought rises up beside it. Doesn't love behave in the very same way?

As these reflections arose within me, they deepened and led me, gradually, to the realization that I might describe my whole life-journey as "learning to love." This was not a sentimental journey but one that led me to myself, to who I truly was, and am, and want to be.

This came to expression in response to a request by Christy Korrow, editor of *LILIPOH*, a quarterly publication which describes itself as "featuring an anthroposophic approach to health; encompassing holistic therapies, preservation of childhood, education, the arts, community, agriculture, nutrition and social renewal." Issue 47, Volume 12, Spring 2007 focused on "Older and Wiser: Honoring our Elders." And, it was for this issue that I was asked to contribute from my perspective as an elder to the

In my early 90s

meaning of old age. My contribution was included under the title: "Learn to Love/And Other Thoughts from Henry Barnes" and, as it bears directly on the present theme, I include it here, with *LILIPOH*'s permission. And it may be of interest to know that the preceding page in the same issue is devoted to the Fellowship Community as described by Miriam Karnow, one of its most active coworkers.

"As I look back on this long life that began on August 12, 1912, on Manhattan Island in the heart of New York City, I have gradually come to realize that the lesson, one might say, which I was born to learn might be expressed as "to learn to love." This may sound sentimental, but I don't mean only romantic love. I mean the ability to enter with one's whole self into every thought, every observation, and into every decision and subsequent action that one undertakes. I believe that this contributes not only to one's mental and psychological health, but also to one's physical and emotional health. And in this connection I would like to express my appreciation and gratitude for the "home for the elderly" of which both my wife and I were—and I still am—resident members. We both joined the Rudolf Steiner Fellowship Community in 2001 and it was here that my wife, Christy Barnes, passed away in December 2002. To conclude, I would say that, as we enter old age, the most important thing is to remember that it is never too late to learn, to change, to grow, and, to learn to love."

But, as I live and wrestle with this realization I come to recognize that love is like the light without which we would be blind, yet which we do not "see" until it strikes an object—a tree trunk, or a boulder, or a human being—and only then do we come to truly "see" and come to know it.

* * *

Because of this, an autobiography is far less about "me," its author, than about the human beings, and experiences, without which, and without whom I could never have become the one I truly am. I need to share the paths that led me to them, but it is *they* who truly enabled me to become myself. With this in mind, I include a brief biography of my wonderful life-companion, Christy MacKaye Barnes, as well as the memorial tributes of our children, John and Marion, to their mother, after her death in December 2002.

Christy MacKaye Barnes

And when I dwell in spirit depths
The ground swell of my soul now flooded
With the heart's warm worlds of love,
My empty indulgences and self-delusions
Are filled with the World Word's fiery power.

In these words Christy Barnes translated the verse by Rudolf Steiner that characterized the week of her birth within the year-long conversation between the human soul and the ever-changing world of nature. The fifty-two verses of *The Calendar of the Soul* were composed by Rudolf Steiner in 1912, when Christy was three years old. It was as if, in that verse, Steiner strove to describe the elements of the child's being which would unfold over the ninety-four years of her earthly biography—"The heart's warm worlds of love" and the "World Word's fiery power"—which Christy, in her innate modesty, felt would fill the "empty indulgences and self-delusions" of her soul.

Those who came to know Christy MacKaye—later, Christy MacKaye Barnes—know that her gentle, loving, poetic artist soul was imbued with a determined will which came to expression in the timing of her arrival on earth, in her choice of family, and in her place of birth.

Christy was expected at Christmas, 1908, but she evidently decided she needed more time and she actually arrived on January 10, 1909. Poetry, drama and imagination were to be the essence of her life, and the MacKaye-Homer-Morse inheritance was what she needed. The hilly countryside of Cornish, New Hampshire, overlooking a wide river valley toward distant mountains with a majestic monadnock, Mt. Ascutney, in the foreground was the place she wanted to call home. There, in their "wayside" home, Christy was welcomed with delight by her sister

Arvia and big brother Robin and was lovingly embraced by her wonderful mother, Marion Homer Morse MacKaye and was immediately enrolled in the dramatic destiny of her poet-playwright, intense, tempestuous and loving Papa, Percy Wallace MacKaye.

Cornish was the wonderland of Christy's earliest years. Barefoot in the summer meadows; snowshoed on the icy fields of winter, and, in the evenings, cozily snuggled on one or another lap beside the open fire to hear her mother weave the never-ending adventures of the two squirrels, Gypsy and Kips. She was swept and tossed and terrified by the breathtaking dramas of her Papa's readings. She was three years old when she watched Ben Jordan and other local carpenters build the house which was to be her "Cornish home" for the rest of her life, looking out over the pasture toward Ascutney and the distant Green Mountains of Vermont.

It was in the same year, 1912, that the family moved to Cambridge for the winter and the little three-year-old experienced urban life. There followed years of city winters and, eventually, also school, private schools in company with elegant girls from affluent homes, so different from the "ups-and-downs"—from "cheesecloth to ermine, and back again"—characteristic of the life of the MacKayes. By the time Christy was fourteen she was in her fourteenth school! Her high school years were blessed by a wonderful teacher of English and literature— Agnes Delano—with whom Christy formed a lifelong connection. Then on to Smith College for two years, followed by two years at Rollins College in Winter Park, Florida, where Percy had been offered a "Poet-in-Residenceship." It was at Rollins that Christy met two college-mates who became lifelong friends: John Gardner, and Carol Hemingway, younger sister of Ernest Hemingway. Christy recounted how the three friends would sit on the dormitory verandah, smoking their corncob pipes and earnestly discussing Emerson, Thoreau, Melville, Whitman and others who carried the torch of creative idealism and imagination in 19th century America.

Before Christy's college years, however, Rudolf Steiner had already entered the consciousness of the MacKaye family. It was

Arvia who first heard about Rudolf Steiner from Irene Brown, an artist-friend of her aunt Hazel MacKaye. In the summer of 1920, Arvia helped Irene Brown care for her two adopted sons, and she was impressed by all that Irene told her about Rudolf Steiner whom Irene had met in Europe before the first World War. Three years later, in 1923, Arvia was chosen to be one of seven American students to go to Europe to meet their counterparts in the German Youth Movement to help foster peace and reconciliation. On this trip, Arvia had the opportunity to cross the border into Switzerland and to hear

Christy and Arvia as Children

Rudolf Steiner speak at the Goetheanum in Dornach. She was deeply impressed, and it was, once again, Irene Brown who made it possible for Arvia to spend several months with her in Dornach. Arvia had two personal interviews with Dr. Steiner and was able to participate in the Christmas Foundation Meeting of 1923/24.

Christy was fourteen at this time and everything she heard from Arvia, after her return, awoke the longing in her to share in these experiences. This opportunity came in the summer of 1928 when Christy and Arvia were present for the opening of the second Goetheanum (the first Goetheanum having been destroyed by fire on New Year's Eve 1922/23). The experience which impressed Christy most strongly on this occasion was the power of the spoken word, both individually by the Goetheanum actors, and in choral recitation by the Speech Chorus under Marie Steiner's direction. This experience kindled in Christy the determination to enter the speech training at the Goetheanum. It was also at this time that Christy joined the Anthroposophical Society.

Two years later, in 1930, Christy became a published poet. A tiny booklet, entitled *Out of Chrysalis* was published as number seven in the series of Vest Pocket Poets by the Angel Alley Press in Winter Park, Florida, with a beautiful frontispiece: a woodcut print by Christy's brother Keith (Robin) MacKaye. This tiny volume contains fourteen poems, and their author was welcomed by the Editor, Edwin Osgood Grover, into the company of American poets. In his Foreword, Professor Grover wrote: "In this tiny volume the author comes 'out of chrysalis' —to join the singing throng. There is youth here, and beauty, combined with a freshness that is prophetic of things to come." And the "things to come" came quickly! In the following year, 1931, Harper & Bros. published *Wind in the Grass* by Christy MacKaye with an introductory letter by the well-known poet Edwin Arlington Robinson. Writing from Peterboro, N.H. on September 21, 1930, Robinson said:

> "Dear Christy,
>
> It has been a great pleasure for me to read these poems of yours in manuscript, and it gives me pleasure of another sort to tell you that I find in them the presence of something for which there is no name in the dictionaries.
>
> Whatever it is, it has a quality that is unusual and intangible, and one that makes all the difference between poetry and mere verse. In these poems there are many flashes of a real imagination, by which I mean the imagination that comes apparently from nowhere, and brings with it something that we did not have before."

Wind in the Grass was built around the four elements: Earth/Water/Air and Fire. Here is a poem from the first section:

The Cry

The cry of a train at night
Makes me hold my breath
Like the sudden glimpse of a terrible dream
Of a beautiful death.

Like the glow of a high-piled thunder cloud
Triumphant in the sun—
The fierce desire for unknown things
That can never be won.

It was during these years that Christy paid a visit to Ireland, walked the Irish countryside with a friend, Kit Buckles, drank in the Celtic soul, and in Dublin experienced the Abbey Players, visited Lady Gregory, met Yeats, and discovered and recognized the native Celt in her own being.

Back home, Christy tried her hand, briefly, at teaching. First in the fledgling Rudolf Steiner School and then at a girls' high school in Washington, D.C. But it was her visit to Dornach that kindled the longing to train in the art of the spoken word. She enrolled in the Speech School under the direction of Marie Steiner, and had the joy of studying under two outstanding teachers: Herthe Hasse and Erna Grund. Christy supported herself by translating and helping with the editing and production of the English-language edition of the weekly magazine *Das Goetheanum*.

Christy back from Ireland

During the early thirties, it came about that all three of the MacKaye children were in Europe. Robin, a gifted writer, poet, dramatist and graphic artist, had suffered a severe accident in 1922 while an undergraduate at Harvard. This had finally led to a breakdown which made it impossible for him to pursue what had promised to be a creative life in the arts. He was left stranded—as a young married man with a fine wife and two lovely children—in need of guidance, of care and healing. This was a terrible blow to his parents, especially to his father, who had seen in Robin his literary heir and the scion of the gifted Clan MacKaye. For Marion MacKaye Robin's breakdown meant the double burden, not only of caring for Percy, but now of Robin as well. They desperately sought the help Robin needed, but every attempt ended in disappointment. Meanwhile Arvia had learned of a sanatorium in South Germany, not too far from Dornach, which seemed to offer the kind of inner and outer help Robin needed, help which he had not found at home. Arvia convinced her parents to try this as a last hope. The necessary financial help was forthcoming, but how was Robin to get to Europe? He would not be able to make the trip alone.

Destiny intervened. As has been mentioned, while at Rollins College, Christy had become friends with John Gardner and Carol Hemingway. It was just at this time that Carol was in Europe and John longed to join her there, but lacked the financial resources to enable him to make the trip. John and Robin already knew each other from the time when Robin lived with John's father, Osa Gardner, who provided him a temporary home until a more permanent solution could be found. In this way, it came about that John Gardner accompanied Robin to Europe where he became a patient of Dr. Husemann at Sanatorium Wiesneck, where he gradually recovered his inner balance and health.

With their three children in Europe and with a commission for Percy to write a biography of Robert Burns, Percy and Marion—once again—set out for the "old country." They spent the winter of 1936/37 in Dornach which led to the poet-friendship between Percy MacKaye and Albert Steffen. The fruit of this friendship was the volume of their inter-translated poems *Im Andern Land – In Another Land*, published in 1937 by Verlag für Schöne Wissenschaften, Dornach, Switzerland. Percy also realized that the Goetheanum as a world center for the arts and as a School of Spiritual Science, uniting science and the arts in a spiritually grounded striving, was a fulfillment both of his own lifelong dream, as well as of his father's Steele MacKaye. At this time, Christy was studying speech in Dornach, where I met her in the summer of 1936. The accompanying photograph was taken two years later when Christy and her parents visited me in England.

It was on June 1, 1939, that Marion MacKaye

With Marion, Christy, and Percy

crossed the threshold of death in St. Germain-en-Laye, just outside of Paris, where she and Percy were visiting Gordon Craig. Following Marion's death, Percy returned to Dornach where he spent the months leading up to the outbreak of the war, as well as the first nine months of the war that followed.

It had been on March 30 of the previous year, 1938, that Arvia and Christy, who were then on their way to Paris to visit their parents, were able to be present in Stuttgart at the closing of the Waldorf School by order of the National-Socialist government. (The Anthroposophical Society and the Christian Community had already been forbidden several years before.) Christy and Arvia experienced the event of the school's closing—the great hall packed with students, former students and parents—not only as a tragedy, but also as a celebration of the spirit of the School which might be closed by a power from outside, but which, inwardly, could not be destroyed.

On the very next day following the closing, Hitler came through Stuttgart on his triumphant return from the annexation of Austria. Arvia and Christy witnessed the event from the front steps of the railway station. Their impression of "Der Führer" as he stood in his open touring car, his arm outstretched in the Nazi salute, was of "an empty shell of a human being."

As described earlier (see p. 25), it was amidst the turbulence of this historic drama that Christy and I were married on September 5, 1939. And it was on June 1, 1940—the first anniversary of Marion MacKaye's death—that the assembled MacKaye/Barnes family sailed from Genoa on the last American ship to leave the Mediterranean, landing in New York on June 10, the day Italy declared war!

On her way to join the family before sailing, Christy was able to visit Marie Steiner in Beatenberg, Switzerland, where Frau Dr. Steiner had taken refuge when it appeared likely that Germany would invade the northwest corner of Switzerland to circumvent the French Maginot Line fortifications and attack France. Through this chain of circumstances, Christy received her Speech School diploma directly from Marie Steiner's hands.

* * *

At home, once more, in America, I joined the faculty of the Rudolf Steiner School in New York City until I was drafted in 1943. In 1952, when our daughter Marion entered kindergarten, Christy met the class she was destined to lead through sixth grade. As indicated earlier, elementary school discipline was not Christy's strength, but nevertheless, several enduring friendships emerged between the students and their teacher before she was "released" to teach in the high school!

During the nearly twenty years Christy was active in the high school—in addition to her life as mother and housewife—she continued

Christy as a high school teacher

her own work as poet and writer, and was an active, productive editor. Her leadership in developing and guiding the high school literary magazine, *The Key*, was one of her important contributions during these years. She also edited the Rudolf Steiner School Association's Newsletter, *Education as an Art*, which was followed by her work on behalf of the Anthroposophical Society as editor of the magazine *Journal for Anthroposophy* from 1974 to 1985.

Christy in Hillsdale

In 1977, Christy and I retired from the Rudolf Steiner School and moved permanently to Hillsdale, N.Y. where we had built a house on Karl and Arvia's property, overlooking an open, friendly valley which was part of the neighboring farm. Here we lived the contented life of a retired couple until John and Astrid convinced us that the time had come to move to Harlemville where the "old folks" could have the help they needed close at hand. And, to back up this good advice, John—with the whole family's help—converted his barn into an attractive bungalow, attached to his own red house by a breezeway, where we could be comfortable and cared for, yet with a sense of independence. This brought us into the heart of the Harlemville community, which we both enjoyed. High school students from the Hawthorne Valley School next door became our household helpers, coming in after school to prepare supper and help with the chores. These young people became part of the family and real friends.

In the autumn of 1996, two friends from Minnesota who wanted, above all, to be at school together, found their way to Hawthorne Valley. Kirsten Bergh and Nina Dietzel became our after-school helpers and good friends. Just before Thanksgiving, they met their death in an automobile accident, which literally threw Kirsten into Nina's arms. Their death was a powerful experience for their schoolmates and friends and is echoed in Christy's poems which follow here:

Kirsten

Black braids and beautiful,
bright and dark shining eyes
brimful of glad surprise,
welcoming warm,
eager to speak to me,
speaking your heart's gold core,
affirming your destiny.
There on the spirit's shore
God guards you from harm.

Nina

Nina, you carry us all in your heart
And bring us together so we may not part.
You fill us with thoughts
that can nourish the soul,
and heap food in each bowl
until healthy and whole
we can follow your feet
to a practical goal.
You're at home with rough weather
and spiders and snow,
and smile on our ways
wherever we go.

Deep in the wise silent center of you
you shed love and strength
on all that we do.

Christy and I in Harlemville

In the early 1940s Arvia had founded the Adonis Press with the special intention of publishing the works of the Swiss poet-dramatist, Albert Steffen, in English translation. After Arvia's death on January 4, 1989, Christy carried on the Press, as well as taking on the challenging task of finally editing and preparing for publication the remarkable biography of their parents, Percy and Marion MacKaye, on which Arvia had been working for the last thirty years of her life. Originally published by Kennebec River Press through the initiative of Bond and Thea Wheelwright, with Arvia's death, followed by Bond Wheelwright's, Adonis Press became the "virtual" publisher, and it was Christy who saw this monumental undertaking through to completion. For anyone who wants to share in, and understand, the destinies and transformations which came to expression in the lives of Percy and Marion MacKaye, *The Power of the Impossible* provides a wonderfully perceptive insight.

It was during the time in which *The Power of the Impossible* was in process of publication that Christy was inspired to prepare a volume which could offer the insight, the help and support so needed by the individual today who stands face to face with the mystery of death. As Christy and her co-editor, Janet Hutchinson, wrote in their foreword to *The Up-Rising in Dying,* "This book has arisen out of the wish to serve the growing awareness and need, and out of the conviction that poetry has the subtlety, imagination and heart forces to illuminate the mystery and stature of this universal event and to help and give strength and courage to those who approach it."

Behind this work, and living through it, is Christy's love for the spoken word which found expression in her devotion to the celebration of the festivals, especially the festival for the dead. Traditionally, this festival took place on All Souls' Day, November 2, the day after All Hallows, whose true meaning has been virtually forgotten in the celebration of Halloween—a caricature of a true festival for those who have died. In New York, Harlemville and at the Fellowship, just a few weeks before her own passing, Christy shared in, inspired, and directed speech choruses in celebration of the reality of death as "rebirth" in the spirit. Many of the poems—especially those by Rudolf Steiner—included in *The Up-Rising in Dying*—had been spoken as part of these festivals. It was the editors' hope that this anthology might inspire others to take similar initiatives. About this, they wrote in their foreword: "These festivals can help to heighten the awareness of the connection between the living and the so-called dead in an entire community."

As artist/editor/publisher, Christy's work on this volume penetrated right into the design and execution of its cover. She and the artist Van James collaborated, and the result was a slant-stroke design which spoke to the eye of an uprising life force through the contrast of yellow-gold with a deep, clear blue. The fact that the book went through a second printing just four years after its publication is witness that it truly filled a need.

The Up-Rising in Dying was followed in 1994 by Christy's own poems: *A Wound Awoke Me.* Carol Katz Williams, a former student of Christy's in the Rudolf Steiner School, writes of this volume in a special issue of the School's Newsletter (Winter 1994/95) dedicated to Christy in celebration of her 85th birthday. Carol writes:

"The poems in this collection were written over nearly fifty years and are grouped in a series of chapters quite disparate in theme and tone: 'Wound and Waking,' 'Choruses' (intended for speech chorus), 'In the Shadow of the Machine Age,' 'Infancy to Old Age,' and others. As is sometimes the case in collections that are taken from a lifetime of work, a sense of biography emerges. One feels one is watching a consciousness unfolding, wonders how and if the poet will reconcile all the elements and contradictions that make up experience.

"This poet does not shrink from the attempt; she takes on the irreconcilables with passion, doubt, anger and depression as well as serenity and praise. Nor does she deny the difficulty:

> Poetry has never sprung
> Up gladly from the neat and guarded mind.
> Cowslips wind their roots in rankest mud;
> The Holy Spirit breeds—in human blood.
> (From "Not Alone From Clarity")

"There is sometimes a guiding theme throughout: poetry itself, the struggle to transform experience, the redemption of suffering in the word. … Many of the poems are embedded in highly structured forms, traditional, or of the poet's own invention. In these poems structure is not distancing or archaic. Instead, meter and rhyme bring measure to feeling that might otherwise overwhelm. … One of the most powerful poems in the collection, 'Cross,' speaks directly to, and through the dynamic use of poetic form:

> Upon the upright beams of rhyme
> Fix the meter's arms, spread wide.
> Upon this strict cross speech may climb
> And the Word be crucified
> Till its mortal parts have died
> And in majesty it ride
> Upward on the spirit's tide,
> Over spacc and over time
> And in Christ be deified.

"When Yeats wrote his exquisite lyric about old age, he was a young man. Christy Barnes wrote her 'Old Age' in old age with the freshness and music of youth:

> Silver-gold moon
> In the rose-blue sky—
> Breath of my childhood
> Blowing by.
> Gold of my heart's core, glowing within,
> Holds my old age in its silvering rim.
> Over and over, the flux and flow
> Of our loving speech as we die and grow.
>
> Wonder and wonder, you and me,
> And the glinting fires of our destiny.

"At the beginning of this year"—Carol Williams concludes her observations—"a group of Christy Barnes' former students gathered to honor her 85th birthday. We spoke of the openness of her perception, which freed us to see ourselves, the loving heart that gave us confidence to embrace the world, the extraordinary range, power and music of her speech that led us to detect a world beyond the world we knew. It is a joy to relate that those who have never met that openness and love and heard the subtle singing of that voice will encounter them, distilled and transformed, in the poems in this book."

Arvia was not only Christy's older sister and friend, she was a guiding presence in the life and destiny of her entire family. And she was actually much more. She was one of those pioneering individualities through whom Anthroposophy—a truly contemporary knowledge of the spirit—was able to take root on the American continent, to grow, blossom and bear fruit. We owe it to Christy that she recognized this and—soon after Arvia's death—wrote, compiled and published a brief, but significant, biographical sketch of Arvia's life and work.

What led, decisively, to this initiative, was the discovery among Arvia's papers of the two meditations, already referred to, given her by Rudolf Steiner, but also Arvia's record of the near-death experience which she had undergone, following a severe illness, in the summer of 1930, when she was twenty-eight years old. Arvia had once spoken with Christy about this experience, but, apparently with no one else, except, in all likelihood, with Karl Ege, her husband. Christy consulted Jörgen Smit, member of the Leadership Council (Vorstand) of the General Anthroposophical Society, who was, at that time, on a visit to this country, in relation to the appropriateness of publishing both the meditations and the near-death experience. Jörgen Smit encouraged Christy to do so, if it could be done in a suitable context. The result was that in 1995 the Adonis Press published Christy's book beautifully illustrated with photographs of Arvia from childhood into old age, together with photographs of examples of her work, both in sculpture and in black and white drawings. Some of Arvia's most significant poems and her characterization of what she saw the world would face at the end of the twentieth century were also included.

It should be noted that the free graphic forms on the front and back covers of this volume are examples of Arvia's work in the field of the graphic arts in which Rudolf Steiner was a challenging innovator. In a foretaste of the work to follow, Christy provides a charming introduction to the "Contrasts and Contradictions" which were characteristic of Arvia. These were then followed by a fifteen-page biographical life sketch in which Christy also describes Arvia's role in helping to bring about the Hawthorne Valley initiative in Harlemville, New York, which was especially close to Arvia's heart in her final years. An aspect of this initiative that might well be renewed were the Artistic Method Workshops, which Christy then largely carried forward after Arvia's death. Characteristic for this initiative was that the participants worked together in three different arts before gathering to seek the ideas implicit in their common experience. These workshops continued over a period of years. Eurythmy and speech were always part of what went on.

The slender volume in which Arvia Ege's life is portrayed is not only a tribute to a highly significant individual of her time, but also to the perceptivity and skill of its author and compiler.

In 1996 a volume was published by the Anthroposophic Press, in collaboration with the Association of Waldorf Schools of North America (AWSNA), under the editorship of Douglas Gerwin, *For the Love of Literature/A Celebration of Language and Imagination.* Its first section was devoted to Christy Barnes' work as a teacher, and its second section contained contributions from a number of individuals, including Francis Edmunds, Cecil Harwood, and Dorit Winter, herself a former student of Christy's in high school. Part One is introduced by the following Foreword by Christy:

"Such articles of mine as are included here have to do with the results of one teacher's work. The most productive aspects of these were inspired by ideas from the work of Rudolf Steiner. The way in which the lessons they tell about evolved—sometimes suddenly, sometimes through long, hard work—and how they were pruned and re-shaped brought about in me something of the joy that accompanies the writing of a poem, especially in the struggle to combine and balance strict form and the fire and chaos of enthusiasm.

"A similar joy came from watching and helping the students likewise invigorate, prune, shape and re-shape their work. More than anything else, I wanted to convey to young people how thinking, augmented to imagination, can become a clear, accurate instrument for perceiving an ever greater depth, breadth and height of reality.

"My hope is that anything I have done may serve as a spark to kindle or inspire others in their struggles to make their own discoveries and to bring young people to discover *their* own abilities and bring to expression the questions and answers concerning the meaning of life which live half-consciously within them."

This Foreword is followed by "A Conversation with Christy MacKaye Barnes" by Andree Ward on behalf of the *Hawthorne Valley Newsletter.* Christy responds to three questions: "How did the work with speech come to carry this central importance for you?" "What was your experience of the speech training at the Goetheanum in Dornach, Switzerland, and who were your teachers?" and "You taught for many years at the Rudolf Steiner School in Manhattan. How did you bring this love of language into your teaching?"

Christy concluded her response to the third, and final question in these words:

> … "In their writing I tried to teach my students not self-expression but the subtle and exact expression of the world about them, and that the use of imagination is to see more deeply, truly, and comprehensively into life: to see in a deed its consequences, and in a human being his inmost or her inmost nature.

> "In looking at the artists of today, I am grateful for those who want to help humanity. Artistic gifts deteriorate if they are not used for an ideal. True art demands tremendous discipline."

To convey a sense for the nature and range of the themes with which Christy dealt in the nine essays that comprise Part One of this volume, their titles are listed below:

> Can Imagination be Trained?—Poetry, Music and Imagination—The Crisis of the Word Today—Speech as Awakener and Healing Force—Poetry: Nourishment and Medicine—Why Write?—Literature and the Drama of Polarities—Schooling Capacities through the study of Great Authors—Backgrounds for Russian Literature.

As she entered her ninetieth year, Christy, with the insight and skilled help of Joel Kobran as co-editor, went to work on a volume of English translations of Albert Steffen's poems. In the pages of *The Power for Resurrection's Flight* one meets Albert Steffen, not only as poet, but as dramatist, artist, stage designer, and as a deeply searching essayist. Writing about Steffen as lyric poet, Rudolf Steiner describes him in the following words:

> "His poetic works have their source in that region of the soul where world-secrets are beheld and human riddles are experienced. But the spirit who is able to see and experience there—daring the depths of the

abyss, often swinging up into starry heights—remains always a molder of images, a tone-creator and is nowhere misled into the frost of mere ideas. Steffen paints with words. The words have color. And the colors have an effect similar to those of paintings which have survived the centuries and proven their true worth. His lyrics come often from the mountains, but from their mountain birthplace have wandered across the plains as spring waters do which have become rivers. They still bear within them their mountain origin, but on the level lands that lend them serenity, they mirror the sun, and magically conjure up there the reflection of the moonlight and of the stars for the souls of those who breathe them in and enjoy them. They murmur and resound with the mysteries of nature, and their reverberation and murmuring becomes, as it is heard, a well-known language."

As is evident in the following translation, Christy was fully able to capture this quality of Steffen's poems:

Easter

Here on earth Christ rises everywhere!
See his guiding, speaking gestures there
In the clouds, in colors, air, and stone,
Shining lovingly in light and tone!

Sense how boulders heave Him from the grave,
How the clouds lift Him aloft toward heaven,
How the wind's waves waft His words along,
How colors glisten with His glance and song!

Raise yourself, O Man, up from your fall!
On the rainbow, mount into the All,
Seize the sun-disc and the sickle moon!
Build your mortal body by their tune.

In the years remaining to her, Christy selected and gathered hitherto unpublished poems of her own, which might make up a final volume of her collected works. Following Christy's death in December 2002, her son John Barnes published these and other poems in a volume entitled: *Imagination's Music/From Youth to Old Age*. Here is a poem from that collection:

Tide

The tide is on the last floor of the sand:
No vestiges of playing feet tomorrow,
Or scamper of white crab, or bird, or wind—
Tomorrow a pristine mirror for the sun
And for the first delighting child
Unbroken worlds to mark.

O tide be on me—more than sleep.
More than forgetfulness, that never can renew,
Be the long surge of memory in one wave
Bearing the force and substance of the sea
To sweep and knead new ledge, new beach for me!

On Sunday, January 19th, 2003, friends gathered in the hall of the Hawthorne Valley School, in Harlemville, in a festive Memorial for Christy. In order to bring this biographical sketch of Christy's life back to Christy herself, John and Marion, Christy's son and daughter, have agreed that the words they spoke for Christy at her Memorial may be included here. With their loving words of appreciation, the long, creative life which embodied "the heart's warm worlds of love" together with "the World Word's fiery power" was fittingly celebrated.

Thoughts about my mother at her Memorial
(John Michael Barnes)

How a person dies can reveal a great deal about how they have lived. I have often experienced the death of someone I have known as a culmination of their life, as a blossoming forth of their being.

I reached my mother's bedside about half an hour after she had passed away. She had died peacefully and lay reclined upon her bed. Her eyes and mouth were open. Her large ears also seemed to be open and listening. Her whole expression was one of wonder and awe, as though she were looking into a world that lay beyond anything she had ever imagined. Many of us had seen a similar open-mouthed, wide-eyed, awe-struck expression on my mother's face at the appearance of an unexpected visitor or when she opened a special birthday present.

A sense of wonder was the source of much of my mother's poetry. I remember how deeply she was taken by a book of thousands of photographs of snowflakes—each one different from the others—or how she wondered at the forms and colors of the blossoms in our flower garden. Wherever she lived, she hung a prism in her window in such a way that the rainbow colors of the sun's spectrum fell upon the wall of her room. She fairly drank in the pure gold, green, blue, violet, the orange, and red. She said the colors nourished and healed her. She was also deeply awed by the power of language. I will never forget her reading a passage from Moby Dick describing the silvery sea by moonlight with the "soft, suffusing seethings" of the waves in the distance.

When I returned to my mother's bedside the next morning her eyes and mouth had been closed. Over the course of the day an entirely new expression spread over her face: A broad smile of love cast a breath of beauty over her emaciated features. I recalled the words of a former student who said she had the opposite of the "evil eye." Unlike the critical, fearsome gaze of some teachers who are quick to point out their students' failings, my mother beheld their deepest potential and drew it forth, eliciting their best efforts. She often in her poems spoke of the sunlike quality of the human heart, of the Christ-sun, and she strove to realize this quality in her own life and especially in her relationship with her students. As her son, I can say that she always gave me her unconditional love. Never did I experience rejection from her.

When I came to see my mother on the third day after her death, her smile was gone. At first I had the impression that her soul was now so distant that her face no longer reflected any aspect of her being. But as I looked more intently I realized that what had seemed to be a total lack of animation was actually the expression of profound peace. It was perhaps the same peace that she felt when she gazed upon the massive peak of Mt. Ascutney from her Cornish home. From what place in her did this deep peacefulness emanate?

As a child Christy was the fastest runner in her class. She was also an excellent swimmer. I can remember the relaxed and powerful strokes of her crawl. She seemed utterly at home in the water. As a student in the speech school in Dornach she embarrassed her male counterparts in Greek gymnastics by wrestling them to the ground. She had a tenacious and determined will. All those in her speech chorus know how many phone calls she made to arrange rehearsals. She simply would not allow any obstacles to deter her. And every detail of the performance was determined —nothing was left to chance. Her family remember her 500 steps: training for the stairs to her beloved bedroom during her last summers in Cornish. We remember how she filled her afternoons or evenings patiently working at her puzzles or reading Joseph C. Lincoln novels for the umpteenth time. It was, I feel, the presence of this deepest aspect of her being that could be felt around her and was reflected in her features on this third day, the day of her funeral celebration.

My Mother
(Marion MacKaye Ober)

In thinking about what I wanted to say, it became clear that I would speak about an inner biography of my mother and her relationship to me; about the ways in which she helped me to lead my own life and prepared both herself and me for her own death. Needless to say, this is hard to put into words, let alone within the space of a few minutes, but I will try.

A picture emerges for me of an arc which starts with the first years of my life, and ends with the last years of my mother's life. In both cases it is particularly the evenings that we spent together that come forward most vividly. The evenings which marked the beginning of the night in which Mom was so awake and inwardly active.

When I was a small girl, she sang to me every night before I went to bed. The songs spoke of far-off places, of a kind of Celtic longing for freedom and wide open spaces. Later, she taught me poems that gave me a sense of the beauty around me, and of the ever changing rhythms of the imagination. Many of these same songs and poems filled the long nights of her old age, and we shared them again as I helped her get ready for bed during her last summers in Cornish.

There were also two events in my childhood through which my mother directly prepared me to face, and not to fear, death. This gift she gave me in my childhood has stayed with me as a deep experience, and I was able to speak of this to my mother as she died.

The first event was when I was eight years old, when my grandfather died. He was sleeping in a room near to my parents' room and to mine. Both my mother and I heard the great exhaling which was close to his last breath. We both went to his room and I stood close to her while he died. She was able in those few moments to transform something which could have been frightening to an eight-year-old into an experience filled with love and reassurance.

The second event came at the end of my seventh grade; a year in which a classmate of mine had died of leukemia. I had a dream just before leaving for the summer that I, too, would die during the summer and not return in the fall to the city. My mother never tried to make me dismiss the dream; she realized that it was of great importance to me. Instead, she reassured me about what it must be like to die. She wrote a poem for me (which is in *A Wound Awoke Me* titled "For a Child who Fears"), and she made a small cloth pocket for me to wear around my neck, and put the poem into it. I said that poem every night of that summer. It was my first realization of what it means to carry an experience of warmth from an inner sun; the experience she wrote of so often in her poems.

In the last summers we had together in Cornish, we spoke sometimes, as I got her ready for bed, about her growing physical difficulties and about her coming death. Mom did not mind speaking about it. There were even times when we got real giggling fits about something she could no longer do or remember. But it was clear to me that she was consciously preparing herself for whatever illness she might encounter before her death and for death itself. She spent some of the nights (when she was not doing puzzles or reading mysteries) memorizing verses she wanted to have close to her and reading and thinking about the time after death.

She said that her readings had not answered all her questions, and I sensed that she had some unnamed fears. But Mom had an extraordinary kind of courage, which was quiet and worked behind the scenes. She faced life through the deeply transformative powers of her imagination—those she had spent her whole life developing.

And I had the feeling when she died, that there was a true confidence in her dying—a stepping out with the same love of freedom and wide open spaces which she gave me a sense of in the songs she sang to me in my childhood.

And I sensed that when she made the gesture with such effort so shortly before she died of putting her arms around me that it was a gesture of love and embracing, not just for me—but for *all* that she left behind.

* * *

To conclude this "Constellation of Human Destinies" we turn now to Christy's older sister, Arvia MacKaye Ege, who was one of the pioneers who enabled Rudolf Steiner's work to find a home in North America. The brief biographical sketch which follows can be expanded and deepened if one turns to Christy's memorable booklet, *Arvia MacKaye Ege/Pioneer for Anthroposophy*, Adonis Press, 1995.

Arvia MacKaye Ege

Arvia was born on Valentine's Day, February 14, 1902, in New York City as the second child and oldest daughter of Percy and Marion MacKaye. She was an artist in every fiber of her being. It was her aunt, Hazel MacKaye, pageant-director and pioneer in the women's suffrage movement, who recommended her niece to her artist friend, Irene Brown, to help her care for the two boys Irene had adopted during the First World War. Thus it was during the summer of 1920, as a young woman of eighteen, that Arvia first heard from Irene Brown about Rudolf Steiner, whom Irene had met in Europe before the War, and it was everything Arvia heard from Irene about Rudolf Steiner that awoke in her the longing to meet this remarkable individual. When, in the summer of 1923, Arvia was selected as one of seven young American students to meet their counterparts in the German Youth Movement to help support reconciliation and peace, she had the opportunity to cross the border from Southern Germany into Switzerland and to experience Rudolf Steiner as he introduced a eurythmy program in the improvised auditorium on the Dornach hill. Arvia's first impression of Rudolf Steiner is so revealing, both of the individual she experienced and of the sensitive young artist who experienced him that it seems appropriate to share briefly from the description she later included in the booklet describing her experience of the Christmas Foundation Meeting which took place later that year.

> "There was a quiet air of ceaseless labor about him. With a smile of greeting and a ceartain unforgettable gesture which I came to know so well—a slight inclination of the head and hand to the side as if in gracious deference to the friends about him—he walked to the speaker's stand at the center below the stage. His pace was measured, as if he carried his body forward with conscious effort, although at the same time there was a lightness, even eagerness about him. Yet once he was on the small speaker's stand, a complete calm fell about

him. He stood for a moment in deep concentration—one strong hand clasped over the wrist of the other, his eyelids lowered, as if cloaked in a quiet that seemed to descend to primal foundations and there to draw breath. It was, it seemed to me, as if he were listening to the far reaches of the universe and the whole world paused to listen with him.

Then, one by one, like drops from a subterranean spring, his words came clear and strong, slowly at first, then gradually increasing to a steady flow. ..."

Arvia's impression of Rudolf Steiner was so profound that, as she descended the Dornach hill, she remembers that, with every footstep, she inwardly exclaimed: "I will come back!" and come back she did. It was, once again, Irene Brown who enabled Arvia to return to Dornach the following autumn. Irene spent the autumn in Dornach and offered to accommodate Arvia if she could remain in Europe. Arvia persuaded her parents to agree, and she spent the summer in Berlin, working with the Quakers in that still war-torn city, and was then able to join Irene in Dornach the following autumn. With Irene's help, Arvia was able to meet with Rudolf Steiner. On her first visit, she showed him examples of her sculpture. He encouraged her and suggested that she introduce a "eurythmic element" into her work, which she did, and he liked what she had done. It was on this second occasion that Rudolf Steiner wrote out, in English, two meditations for Arvia's personal use. Both of these meditations, in Rudolf Steiner's handwriting, are included in facsimile in the volume which her sister Christy Barnes wrote and compiled, following Arvia's death.

Irene Brown also made it possible for Arvia to be present for the nine days of the Christmas Foundation Meeting which proved to be central in Arvia's whole life experience. Her memories of this event were published in *The Experience of The Christmas Foundation Meeting, 1923*, Adonis Press, 1981.

Arvia returned home to America, and it was in the years which followed that she became a close friend and colleague of Lucy van der Pals Neuscheller who pioneered the first beginnings of eurythmy in this country.

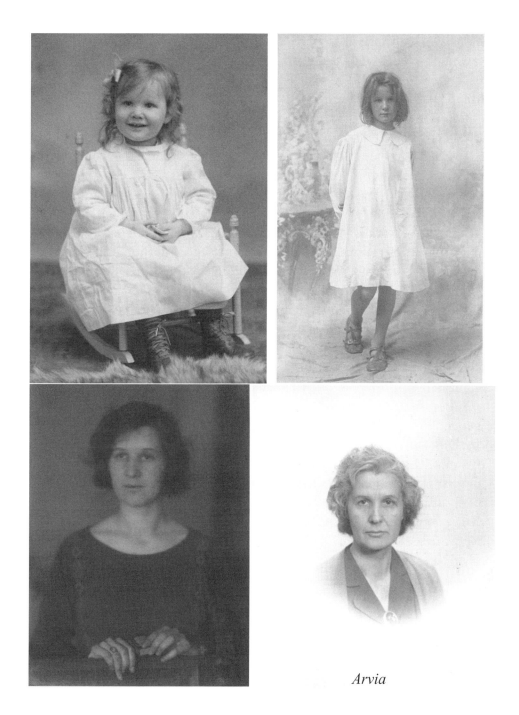

Arvia

It was also with Lucy that Arvia took part in the Old English Nativity play, in which Arvia played the Angel. In 1928 she was one of the five founding teachers of the Rudolf Steiner School—the first Waldorf school in North America—where she taught painting, drawing and handwork.

An example of the insight which Arvia brought to her work as a teacher of art and of practical handwork skills comes to expression in a most remarkable article entitled "The Human Hand, Its Activities and Role in Education." This appeared in a special issue of the *Journal for Anthroposophy* devoted to *Creative Impulses in Waldorf Education*. Beautifully illustrated with photographs of work both by students of Arvia's in the Rudolf Steiner High School, as well as of work by students of Max Wolffhügel in the original Waldorf school in Stuttgart, Germany, this issue deserves to be known not only in Waldorf education but in the broadest circles of educational interest today. It provides an overview of this aspect of a truly human educational curriculum, culminating with a section on *The Human Form*.

When, in 1940, Arvia, together with her father, her brother, Christy and I, was forced by the war to return home from Europe, she again taught at the Rudolf Steiner School. But she also translated two of Albert Steffen's dramas and established the Adonis Press where they were published. In her translations, Arvia sought to recreate the dynamic rhythms and sounds of the original. In later years she translated three of Rudolf Steiner's Mystery Dramas as well as many of his verses and meditations, which were published in 1979 by the Anthroposophic Press in a volume entitled *Truth-Wrought-Words*. A collection of her own poems, expressions of her deep spiritual striving, entitled *The Secret Iron of the Heart*, was published by Adonis Press in 1982. Over a period of 30 years, and with increasing intensity right up to her death, Arvia worked on her extraordinary tribute to her parents: *The Power of the Impossible—the Life Story of Percy and Marion MacKaye*. This crowning achievement of Arvia's life was published after her death in 1989 by her sister Christy.

After the war Arvia was asked to travel to Germany and talk to Karl Ege—the last teacher to be appointed by Rudolf Steiner to the

Arvia teaching

Waldorf School in Stuttgart—and urge him to come to America to help the fledgling Waldorf High Schools. Arvia succeeded, and a friendship developed which led to their marriage in 1950.

Soon thereafter, Arvia and Karl bought a house in Hillsdale, New York. Later, when the farm in Harlemville was purchased only 11 miles away, Arvia and Karl, who had been deeply involved in the initiative from its inception, poured their energies into the founding of what has since come to be known as Hawthorne Valley. Arvia was the chief instigator of the Artistic Method Workshops that took place there each summer for some ten years.

In conclusion it seems appropriate to allow the reader to share in Arvia's experience in the late summer of 1930, when, as a young woman, twenty-eight years of age, she was brought face to face with an experience, the significance of which Rudolf Steiner had prophetically foreseen in observations to which he gave expression on several occasions in the years preceding the First World War, to which we now refer.

It was especially in the year 1910 that Rudolf Steiner spoke of a change in human consciousness which would lead to the awakening of a new capacity for the experience of the etheric world in which Christ was to reappear. This is an event, Rudolf Steiner said, of the utmost significance for our time and for the future of human life on earth, and it is of great importance that this not pass unnoticed by mankind today. He referred to the fact that the awakening to this event would first begin in the 1930s and would then gradually be shared by more and more individuals in the years to come. He spoke of this in a lecture on January 25, 1910, in Karlsruhe, Germany, and on March 6, 1910, in Stuttgart.

In the first of these two lectures, Rudolf Steiner reviews the evolution of the human soul from Atlantean times up to the present day, stressing the pivotal significance of the entry of the Christ Being into human life on earth and what it would have meant for human evolution if this event had passed entirely unnoticed by human beings of that time. He then speaks of the importance that the experience of Christ in the etheric world should not pass unnoticed in our time today. He then goes on to say:

"Today we are living in a similar age. Since Kali Yuga, the Dark Age, ended in 1899, new soul faculties are once again being slowly prepared in a similar way. It is very possible that our contemporaries, those living in our age, may sleep through this. Gradually, we will learn to recognize what needs to take place for all humanity during the age that began at the end of Kali Yuga. It is our task to see that this transitional event does not pass by unnoticed and without affecting human progress.

"Kali Yuga ended only a few years ago, around 1899. We are now approaching a time when, in addition to evolved self-awareness, certain clairvoyant faculties will be regained naturally. ... Although only a small number of people will develop these faculties during the next few decades, spiritual science will spread, because we feel a responsibility toward something that is really happening; it must take place according to the natural course of events. Why do we teach spiritual science? Because phenomena will appear in the near future that only spiritual science will be able to understand; it will be misunderstood without spiritual science.

"In a few people, these faculties will develop relatively quickly. It is true, certainly, that even today people can ascend, through esoteric training, far beyond what is beginning on a small scale for humanity. At the same time, the goal to which we can ascend today through the appropriate self-development is already being prepared somewhat for all humanity. It will be necessary to speak of this, whether people understand it or not, between 1930 and 1940. Only a few decades separate us from the time when such phenomena will be more frequent."

It is because of the great significance with which Rudolf Steiner in 1910 drew the attention of his listeners both in Karlsruhe and in Stuttgart (and also through the translation and publication of these lectures to us as their readers today) that I feel the responsibility to share with the reader of this autobiography the description which Arvia MacKaye wrote of the event she experienced in the late summer of 1930, which my wife Christy MacKaye Barnes and I found at the time of her death almost sixty years later. I will also include Arvia's two poems with which she gave utterance to this life-changing event. In doing so I also hope to draw the reader's attention to the beautiful small volume that Christy wrote and compiled about Arvia, which includes illustrations of many examples of Arvia's graphic drawings and sculptures.

(After a sudden, severe illness in the Adirondack Mountains, when for three days Arvia could hardly move, eat, or speak, the experience written below came to her in the late summer of 1930. The words enclosed in parentheses were written in later by Arvia in 1933.)

I felt myself suddenly freed from my body. I felt it like a skeleton beneath me. As if on wings, I soared upward, mightily. Then I suddenly felt everything that I was belonged to another—belonged to a mighty, winged being—Lucifer. (And then, in this moment, it was taken by him.) And there, in this moment, it seemed to me as if my being was taken by him—as a soul I died—(I was no more). But into this nothing there poured itself a whole world of flooding light and love (unending love) which was at the same time Word and spoke, although not with earthly words. But what was spoken I could only grasp with the earthly words: "I am the Way, the Truth, and the Life. I am no longer to be sought without in the cosmos—I am united with the earth—and I am with you until the end of the world." (The speaking, sounding light was at the same time countless outflowing, outpouring beings, who streamed forth from Him.)

An indescribable happiness filled everything. Below I sensed that which belonged to me as soul and from out it there sprang now a brightly shining radiant child. The flooding (resounding) world began to leave me. Beside me I then saw a gigantic temple and within it the four brothers, as in the Mystery Dramas! This became ever smaller and smaller until it vanished into my body and I found myself again where I lay in the pine forest. Joyful happiness and blissfulness filled me and I felt that the earth was, for me, made new (my life also). (I knew that it was transformed and permeated by His unending love and light.)

I WAS GIVEN A GIFT
1986

The tale I would tell,
Were I truly able to shape it
In all its fullness and form,
Would take my very life,
As it has taken my life to live it.
And yet with each breath
The Giver who gave it
Is seeking to speak it—
So I leave you only this hieroglyph.

Long ago I was given a gift,
When my days were young,
That has lit every step of the way
With a hidden wonder and warmth,
A healing that has cured
Every wound. …
And though my heart cried out aloud to the world,
yet it was muted in silence—
For who can speak
Of such a glory that is not his own. …

But now throughout the long years
And wearying labor—grown old—
The cup that I carry
Has been cooled and cleansed,
Hallowed and wrought,
Till at last, with mercy and grace,
It is empty and sturdy enough
For the sun-warm wine of the Word.
For in utter loss, a shroud was torn apart,
One day, when I was young,
And it was the Sun
Who met my gaze—
The Son of Man and God
Who has taken this planet
Into His Heart
As His home and abode!

And I cannot go to the grave
And enter the hall of the stars
Till my lips have opened
And spoken. …

HE CAME

Let no one say
He did not come—
For in very deed
He came!

Oh heed—
For in heart-rending
Sheer reality
His presence and His Word
Have been seen and heard!

Flooding the gulf of death—He came!
Transfiguring the void—
A sudden sun- and world-appearing,
Spirit-spending
Wonder-speaking One!
Tending, healing, mending,
Uttering, revealing,
In inmost clarity
Of spirit-kindled flame,
The wrath-repealing,
All-redeeming
Miracle and might
Of His sacrifice,
The streaming, life-bequeathing light
Of His free,
Divinely human, death-consuming,
All-consoling Name!

Speech
That was breathed and borne, and bodied
By innumerable light-embuilded beings,

Flocking and eternally descending
As in a soft snowfall
Of starry, seeing eyes and wings.
Sounding, singing, uttering,
Creating, ordering, uncluttering
The void through which they flowed.
And yet, 'twas He who spoke!
With freshening, world-altering,
Sun-structured language.
And with His inmost speech
To each—His loving call
Awoke
The All!

Oh, in this brutal siege
Of dire, computer-ridden dark,
This atom-splintered reign of hate and greed—
That would blind
And bind mankind
As its helpless prey,
May each,
In self-won stillness,
Wake and hark!
Cease all delay.

Draw fresh breath to startle thought and will,
And from the hate-bled, stricken heart
Make that crying, inmost choice—
Free, untarnishable, true,
Which only each can do.

For the fury of the storm of wrath,
Leaving desolation in its path,
Is here!

Yet He is present
As the vast, unfailing day!

Oh, let no one say
He did not come—
For in very deed
He came—
And is ever here!

Thoughts on this Constellation of Destinies

By John Michael Barnes

To one who knew them, it is striking how these three individuals not only had a great deal in common but also were very different and thus complemented each other in significant ways. Let me now attempt to characterize the unique constellation of destinies that arose through their interrelationship.

My father Henry Barnes was endowed with a very strong constitution and abundant life forces. Even in his early nineties he still had the capacity to compile his monumental history of anthroposophy in America, *Into the Heart's Land*. His steady phlegmatic temperament combined with his rigorous self discipline, strong will power and good organizational skills to form formidable working habits. He was also blessed with a powerful intellect, common sense and an excellent memory. With his handsome good looks, his well-balanced, affable nature and his great gift as a public speaker, he was a natural leader. Because of these gifts, his family background, his excellent education and his seven years of preparation in Europe, Henry Barnes was ideally suited to represent Waldorf education and anthroposophy. For decades he was not only chairman of the faculty of the Rudolf Steiner School and a carrying force in the Waldorf movement but also a pillar of the Anthroposophical Society in America. When he wrote about "the third space" (see pp. 51-54), he was writing out of his own experience as a mediator between an esoteric world of spiritual truth and a public world in which every individual is entitled to his or her own opinion.

Arvia, on the other hand, possessed deep spirituality, vision and great artistic gifts. But throughout her life her health—her digestion in particular—was very delicate. She was a night-owl, and during the last decades of her life she worked deep into the night, sleeping only during the morning hours when most people are already at work. As a child she missed the first years of school because of her father's turbulent life as a dramatist. Although she was deeply steeped in literature and had an unusual gift with poetic language, Arvia had difficulty with reading and academic work until she entered college. She had a melancholic temperament and was very serious by nature. Until the end of her life, however, her profound experience of the Christ, of anthroposophy and of Rudolf Steiner, particularly of the Christmas Conference of 1923-24, remained a powerful reality within her that irradiated her inner being with its sunlike substance.

Although her health was poor and she was unable to be very active physically or socially, Arvia had a powerful and determined will, and she followed events with a profound sense of responsibility. It was thus natural for her to form a working relationship with my father in which they would consult about the deeper implications of his work in the "outer world." For practical reasons, these consultations could only take place during the night. Even though it must have been difficult for my father to engage in what must have often been lengthy and intense conversations after a long day's work, it is obvious, judging from my father's great respect for Arvia, that he valued her insight and wisdom. Thus these two very different individuals complemented each other in an extraordinary way. This relationship persisted throughout most of my father's working life as Arvia lived in the same house with our family for many years while my father taught at the Rudolf Steiner School and my parents later moved in next door to Arvia in Hillsdale while they were helping to found what has come to be known as Hawthorne Valley.

My mother, Christy MacKaye Barnes, unlike Arvia and Henry, was the third and youngest child in her family. She therefore did not carry their same sense of responsibility but was more playful in nature. Her life was dedicated to the art of the spoken word, and she succeeded masterfully in conveying its power and beauty to her high school English classes. Though my father was a consummate teacher and never had serious discipline problems, as a high school English teacher my mother was more inspiring, for she had the MacKaye fire, imagination and sense of drama. Though she had a deep sense for the spirituality that can live in anthroposophy, she never thoroughly acquainted herself with its philosophical foundations and conceptual structure. Unlike my father, therefore, she was unable to represent anthroposophy as a public speaker. She did, however, love to give expression to its spiritual substance through the spoken word. She was especially dedicated to the art of choral speech. Here she experienced a deeper, more powerful dimension of the spoken word, and after she retired from teaching she devoted a great deal of her time to preparing speech choruses for seasonal festivals. The All Souls Festival at Hawthorne Valley always featured powerful choral recitations of appropriate texts as long as my mother was able to lead them.

My mother was also committed to her family and friends. She sacrificed much of her own life to help Arvia with practical tasks or to care for her. As a daughter, sister, wife and mother, she endured many hardships for her family. She suffered through her years as an elementary school class teacher. Nevertheless, her health was good and she had the capacity to enjoy life thoroughly. She also succeeded in transforming and transcending the challenges she faced in life through her poetic art.

An important aspect of the close karmic connection of these three individuals is the fact that all three, Henry, Christy and Arvia, met anthroposophy during their youth and spent a number of those formative years in Dornach and in Europe. They then returned to this country to bring the deeply human impulse they had found there back to their native land. Though all three came of old American families and grew up in the United States, they experienced Central Europe as their spiritual home. If asked what was at the heart of their inner convictions, I believe all three would have pointed to the Foundation Stone verse and the accompanying spiritual impulse given by Rudolf Steiner at the re-founding of the Anthroposophical Society at Christmas 1923.